"Countless subjects afflicted with bulimia have already benefited from using the original self-help manual, one of the first written after the description of these disorders. The new edition retains the appeal of the original through a friendly style, moving case-vignettes and ingenious illustrations. Some additions enable the inclusion of new research on the body image disturbance and on refined treatment techniques, while an extra chapter facilitates access to sources of help in different parts of the world. I recommend this book with full enthusiasm."

– Gerald Russell, Emeritus Professor of Psychiatry,
Institute of Psychiatry, King's College London

"Ulrike Schmidt, Janet Treasure and June Alexander make an outstanding team in this second edition of one of the foremost self-help manuals for sufferers with bulimic disorders. Drs Schmidt and Treasure are at the cutting edge in their clinical and research work in this domain, and adding June Alexander to this team provides this edition with an eloquent voice that represents sufferers and carers. This book is a great practical guide for those who are unwell, and also for those of you who are there to guide these individuals through their struggles toward recovery – professionals, families and friends alike."

– Daniel Le Grange, PhD, Benioff UCSF Professor
in Children's Health, University of California, San Francisco, USA

"Getting Better Bite by Bite is a beautifully illustrated step-by-step guide for eating disorders recovery. Through rich storytelling and concrete practical exercises reflecting decades of collective clinical experience, this book accompanies the reader across the stepping stones to recovery. Warmth, compassion, and deep understanding flow from every page integrating perspectives of two of the most respected eating disorder clinicians in the world and a survivor/advocate. This guide avoids jargon and provides solid advice for anyone with an eating disorder. A rich resource for every library and a comforting companion for anyone contemplating recovery."

– Cynthia Bulik, PhD, FAED, Professor,
Karolinska Institutet and the University of North Carolina at Chapel Hill,
author of Midlife Eating Disorders *and* Binge Control

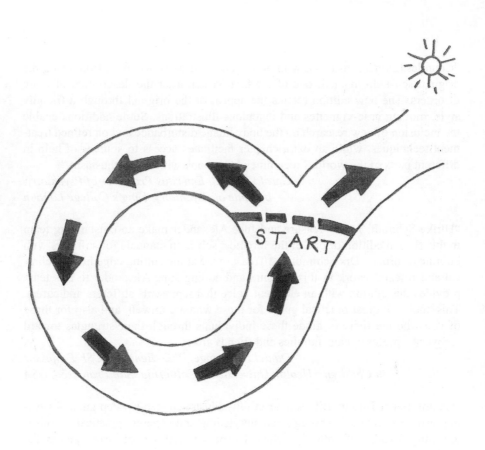

Getting Better Bite by Bite

A survival kit for sufferers of bulimia nervosa and binge eating disorders

Second edition

**Ulrike Schmidt,
Janet Treasure
and
June Alexander**

Routledge
Taylor & Francis Group

LONDON AND NEW YORK

Second edition published 2016
by Routledge
2 Park Square, Milton Park, Abingdon, Oxon, OX14 4RN

And by Routledge
711 Third Avenue, New York, NY 10017

First edition published 1993

Routledge is an imprint of the Taylor & Francis Group, an informa business

© 2016 Ulrike Schmidt, Janet Treasure and June Alexander

The right of Ulrike Schmidt, Janet Treasure and June Alexander to be
identified as authors of this work has been asserted by them in accordance
with sections 77 and 78 of the Copyright, Designs and Patents Act 1988.

British Library Cataloguing-in-Publication Data
A catalogue record for this book is available from the British Library

Library of Congress Cataloging-in-Publication Data
Schmidt, Ulrike, 1955-
   [Clinician's guide to Getting better bit(e) by bit(e)]
   Getting better bite by bite : a survival kit for sufferers of bulimia nervosa
and binge eating disorders / Ulrike Schmidt, Janet Treasure, and June
Alexander. —Second edition.
      pages cm
   Revision of: Clinician's guide to Getting better bit(e) by bit(e). c1997.
   1. Bulimia.   I. Treasure, Janet.   II. Alexander, June, 1950-   III. Title.
   RC552.B84S36   2016
   616.85'263—dc23
   2015012752

ISBN: 978-1-138-79740-6 (hbk)
ISBN: 978-1-138-79737-6 (pbk)
ISBN: 978-1-315-75401-7 (ebk)

Typeset in Times New Roman
by Apex CoVantage, LLC

We thank our patients, whose stories, comments and ideas were invaluable in developing this book.

Contents

About the authors

Ulrike Schmidt is professor of eating disorders at the Institute of Psychiatry, Psychology and Neurosciences at King's College London. She is also a consultant psychiatrist in the Eating Disorders Unit at the Maudsley Hospital. She was a member of the NICE Eating Disorders Guidelines Development Group, chair of the Section of Eating Disorders at the Royal College of Psychiatrists and a board member of the Academy for Eating Disorders (AED). She is a Council member of Beat, the UK's main eating disorders charity. She is the recipient of a 2005 NHS Award for Innovative Service Delivery, the 2009 AED Leadership Award for Clinical, Educational and Administrative Services, the 2013 KCL Supervisory Excellence Award and the 2014 Hilde Bruch Award for Outstanding Achievements in Eating Disorders Research and Treatment. Professor Schmidt has published some 300 peer-reviewed papers and 90 other publications on eating disorders, including text books, chapters, patient manuals, and web-based treatment or training packages. A key focus of her research has been on development of brief scalable psychological treatments for eating disorders.

Janet Treasure, OBE, is a psychiatrist who has worked professionally with people with eating disorders for over 33 years at the Eating Disorder Unit at the South London and Maudsley Hospital NHS Trust, which is a leading centre in clinical management and training of eating disorders. She was chairman of the physical treatment section of the UK NICE guideline committee. She is the chief medical advisor for Beat (the main UK eating disorder charity). She was awarded with a leadership for research with the Academy of Eating Disorders in 2007 and was also awarded a lifetime achievement award from the Academy of Eating Disorders and from Beat in 2014. She is trustee of the charities Student Minds, Charlotte's Helix, Diabetics with Eating Disorders and the Psychiatry Research Trust and is on the scientific board of the charities SUCCEED, MAED – Mothers Against Eating Disorders and FEAST.

June Alexander is a writer and PhD candidate. At age 11, June developed anorexia nervosa and this challenge, together with a love of writing, shaped her life. Upon recovering from her illness at age 55 in 2006, June departed a journalism career to write books about eating disorders – combining life experience and professionals skills to disseminate evidence-based research for health practitioners and mainstream readers. June serves on national and international mental health and advocacy organisations, including Academy of Eating Disorders, F.E.A.S.T. and the National Eating Disorders Collaboration (Australia). Her website and blog supports this advocacy work. She speaks publicly on the theme "Hope at Every Age" and presents workshops on writing as a therapy. June is a PhD candidate in creative writing at CQUniversity, Australia, exploring how diary writing can be therapeutically applied in the treatment of eating disorders, and is a diary-writing mentor with inpatients in a hospital eating disorders unit. June has a website at www.junealexander.com.

Elise Pacquette, illustrator, gains inspiration for her work from her experience of recovery from anorexia nervosa. She understands many of the battles along the journey towards recovery, including the reluctant start, the hurdles, the temptations and the slip-ups. Having made this journey, she appreciates that it not only took her towards recovery but also was rewarding in itself, gathering along the way many insights and an understanding of herself that have been invaluable. Elise is now married with children and, inspired by her eating disorder experience, has developed a course for 11–12 year olds to attend with their parents/carers about growing up and becoming independent; run as an after-school club, this course helps parents and children to explore together what it means to grow up in today's culture. Elise wishes all those who journey through this book the strength to keep going, step by step, bite by bite.

Introduction

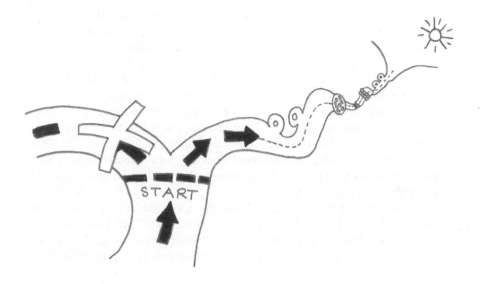

The important message throughout every page of *Getting Better Bite by Bite* is that recovery *is* possible, at every age. This book does not pretend that recovery from an eating disorder is easy. What this book does do is arm you with skills and knowledge to make your recovery journey as smooth and rewarding as possible.

Getting Better Bite by Bite portrays what life is really like, living with bulimia nervosa or binge eating disorder. (Hereafter, we will usually just use the term bulimia). Until directly affected by an eating disorder, most people's perception of these illnesses is obtained from the media. The perception is almost always nothing like reality. There is nothing glamorous or desirable about bulimia or binge eating. Much mystique remains. Misconceptions and misinformation abound about the causes, the health risks and the treatment. Access to treatment is difficult for many sufferers, and friends and relatives often have no idea how to help. Also, some doctors are not sympathetic or understanding, and make the person feel their problem is self-inflicted and trivial and thereby compound the illness characteristics of guilt, shame and loneliness.

This book was originally written for the patients with bulimia attending the Eating Disorders Clinic at the Maudsley Hospital, London. Our patients wanted information about their illness and practical advice on how to overcome their problems. This book contains in condensed form what we know to be the essential ingredients of cognitive-behavioural therapy (CBT), a form of therapy endorsed by the UK's National Institute of Health and Care Excellence[1] as the most effective treatment for bulimia. In addition, it incorporates evidence-based strategies for successfully changing problem behaviours as outlined in the NICE guidelines for Behaviour Change[2].

Getting Better Bite by Bite is unique in several respects. It strongly focuses on enhancing readers' motivation and belief in their ability to change, includes strategies for dealing with common accompanying problems and has an easy-to-read conversational style[3]. The first edition of *Getting Better Bite by Bite*, released in 1993, has helped many eating disorder sufferers, not only at the Maudsley but around the world. We know this because many people wrote to us after working through the book to tell us their personal recovery story and give us feedback. Many people, on reading this book, have felt empowered to tackle their eating problem and, beyond that, to address other difficulties in their lives, too. Some people – often those feeling less sure about what they want – found the book helpful in understanding their problem and gaining tools to make an informed decision about whether or not to enter treatment.

Clinical trials using this book have shown that a significant proportion of people working through this book by themselves make a full and lasting recovery from their eating disorder, and when this book is used with a few sessions of support and guidance from a therapist, it is as effective and more sustainable than a much longer face-to-face CBT treatment[4].

CBT delivered by a therapist typically includes a case formulation in the form of a diagram or map showing how a person's difficulties all "hang together". This can be very helpful, especially if it is really tailored to an individual. However, this approach does not always "hit the spot" for the person if, for example, the map is too complicated or too simple, or makes the person feel forced into an unhelpful structure. The available research evidence suggests that therapists like these diagrams, but it is not clear how helpful or necessary such diagrams actually are for people in overcoming their difficulties[5]. We therefore decided not to put such a diagram into this book. Instead, we have taken a problem-led approach, with each chapter tackling an area relevant to most or particular subgroups of people with bulimia or binge eating.

This updated Second Edition can help you, too, on your journey to recovery. You must undertake this journey of change yourself, but we can be like your support crew, ready to help you plan and prepare and to be beside you as you travel towards your destination. We can provide maps and point out the dangers and pitfalls along the route. Importantly, we can help you find a way to overcome the inevitable obstacles. No matter how big the obstacle, we can help you find a way around it and work with you to achieve recovery. Remember, there is always a solution.

You may have mixed feelings about leaving the sense of security that accompanies the familiar territory of bulimia. You know that there are severe dangers on all sides, and you may have constructed ways of ignoring or suppressing those dangers. You will feel frightened about entering the new territory without the backup of your bulimia or binge eating behaviours. This book is filled with the travellers' tales of people like yourself who have made the journey before you. They are here to travel with you, to keep you company and help to decrease your sense of isolation.

This book is full of clues on how to avoid the traps of self-defeating thought patterns. It contains the tools you need to travel safely along the road to recovery. It shines a light on changes that you can make to replace the short-lived and doomed-to-fail rewards that you get from your illness. *Getting Better Bite by Bite* offers safe, reliable, long-lasting alternatives.

Getting Better Bite by Bite also will help you to anticipate, and prepare for, obstacles and detours on the way. You may experience initial discomfort (just like we get aches when we start a new exercise or dance routine, as latent muscle groups are brought into use), but persevere because eventually you will get past this stage and start to recognize and enjoy the many benefits of your new skills and new-found strengths.

Not everyone is successful at first. Setbacks and lapses commonly occur. However, always remain hopeful because you can learn from these experiences. For some sufferers, the change process is slow and laborious, requiring many attempts before achieving freedom of self; others find the way is easier.

The time taken to recover from bulimia or binge eating disorder is three months on average, but differs for each person. Vigilance and a high level of self-awareness is often necessary for years afterwards to ensure your life remains unshackled by the eating disorder.

You may feel, *"I can't help myself. I have tried. My problem is too severe for this. I need someone else to take over."* However, any form of treatment can work only when you are actively involved. The more you put in, the more you will strengthen and empower your true sense of self. So you might as well start now. We don't expect that reading *Getting Better Bite by Bite* will make you suddenly "snap out" of your problem. However, deciding to do what it takes to stop your chaotic eating pattern is the important first step on a journey that leads to increased freedom and self-esteem.

A few words of caution

Some people are persuaded by their families or partners to work on their problems. This book can help only if YOU really want to get better for YOURSELF. *Getting Better Bite by Bite* can't help if you are not ready to change, or if you just want to change to please somebody else. To assess your readiness for undertaking the recovery journey, go to Chapter 1; fill in your own balance sheet, and keep it close by (in your bag or pocket) for regular consultation wherever you go.

You will be asked to do a lot of hard work over the next few weeks. Even when you are determined to get better, there are bound to be ups and downs. The best way to cope is to take each day as it comes and focus on living in the moment, rather than the past.

You may feel tempted to "binge" on this book, that is, read it quickly and throw it in a corner, telling yourself, *"this is nothing new"*; *"I knew all this, already"*. This is certainly what the eating disorder bully wants you to think. Strive to be honest with, and listen to, your own true self. Take time to absorb and digest each chapter slowly.

What this book can and can't do

Getting Better Bite by Bite can't cure you but can help you acquire new coping skills, so that the eating disorder no longer rules your life. This book is not aimed primarily at helping you to understand why you developed an eating problem. Understanding the underlying causes is often difficult and happens only gradually, if at all. To know what caused the eating problem is important, but rarely helps to change distressing eating symptoms. *Getting Better Bite by Bite* aims to help you develop new skills to ease these symptoms and to help you gain control over your life. Once eating symptoms are addressed, underlying causes often become clearer and a decision will be easier regarding whether you need treatment in your own right.

Notes and references

1   National Institute of Health and Care Excellence, 2004. Eating Disorders: Core Interventions in the Treatment and management of anorexia nervosa, bulimia nervosa and related disorders. http://guidance.nice.org.uk/CG9
2   National Institute of Health and Care Excellence, 2014. Behaviour Change: Individual Approaches (PH49). http://guidance.nice.org.uk/PH49
3   We compared six widely available CBT self-help interventions for bulimia and found that GBBB was by far the most easy and straight forward read (Musiat, P. & Schmidt, U., 2010. Chapter in Agras, W.S. (Ed.), *The Oxford Handbook of Eating Disorders*. Oxford Library of Psychology).
4   *Getting Better Bite by Bite (GBBB)* has been tested in seven clinical trials in the UK and internationally. These trials show that working through the book by yourself is better than doing nothing and waiting for treatment with a therapist. GBBB with guidance from a therapist (8 sessions) is as good as individual CBT (16–20 sessions) (Thiels, C., et al. *American Journal of Psychiatry*, 1998;155:947–953; Treasure, J., et al. *British Journal of Psychiatry*, 1996;168:94–98; Treasure, J., et al. *British Medical Journal*, 1994;308(6930):686–689). GBBB with guidance also has advantages over group CBT (Bailer, U., et al. *International Journal of Eating Disorders*, 2004;35:522–537) and family-based treatment in bulimic adolescents (Schmidt, U., et al. *American Journal of Psychiatry*, 2007;164:591–598). A large trial from Austria has shown that GBBB works as well as Internet-based CBT (Wagner, G., et al. *British Journal of Psychiatry*, 2013;202:135–141). Other researchers using a different self-help book have found that if you start treatment using self-help for bulimia but with the option of adding other treatments (CBT from a therapist and antidepressant medication) if necessary, you do better in the longer term than if you have "Rolls Royce" CBT with a therapist straight away (Mitchell, J.E., et al. *British Journal of Psychiatry*, 2011;198:391–397). We can only speculate why this might be, but it is likely that if you mobilise your inner

resources and think about what *you* can do *yourself*, this is more helpful than waiting for someone else (a therapist) to provide the answers for you.

Finally, we and others have found that working through the book and actually doing the suggested between-session tasks leads to much better outcomes than simply skim reading it (Beintner, I., et al. *Clinical Psychology Review*, 2014;34(2):158–176). This may sound obvious but is crucial.

5   Wilson, G.T. *Behaviour Research and Therapy*, 1996 Apr;34(4):295–314. Moorey, S. *Journal of Cognitive and Behavioral Psychotherapies*, 2010 Mar;38(2):173–184.

1   The way forward

Do I suffer from bulimia?

A mountainous pile of labels has emerged to describe a person who overeats and feels distressed about it. The labels include: compulsive overeating, bulimia nervosa, bulimia, binge eating disorder, bulimarexia, night eating syndrome and loss-of-control eating. They overlap and have an awful lot in common with each other. Problems with overeating can occur in people of any body weight (underweight, average, and overweight). This book has been written for people who fall into any of these categories. If feeling unsure whether any of this fits you, fill in and score the test in Table 1.1.

If your severity index score is 5 points or above, you are likely to have a significant eating disorder at present.

If your symptom score is 15 points or above, you have a lot of the thoughts and attitudes that go with an eating disorder and are clearly distressed by it.

How to use this book

Like many people, you may have the habit of starting to read a book at the end or in the middle, perhaps flicking through the pages until a chapter title grabs your interest. In principle, you can do that with this book, but let us explain a few things first: Chapters 1 to 6 are the core chapters that teach all the steps you need for solving unhealthy eating habits. We suggest you read Chapters 1 to 6 together, but in whatever order you like. These chapters will help you decide whether you are correct in deciding that you want to get over your bulimia and are ready to start the journey.

Table 1.1 Bulimic investigatory test, Edinburgh[1]

Questions	Scores
1. Do you have a regular daily eating pattern? Yes = 0, No = 1	___
2. Are you a strict dieter? Yes = 1, No = 0	___
3. Do you feel a failure if you break your diet once? Yes = 1, No = 0	___
4. Do you count the calories of everything you eat, even when not on a diet? Yes = 1, No = 0	___
5. Do you ever fast for a whole day? Yes = 1, No = 0	___
6. If yes, how often is this? Have once = 1; now and then = 2; once a week = 3; 2–3 times a week = 4; every second day = 5	___
7. Do you do any of the following to help you lose weight? (a) Take diet pills; (b) Take diuretics (water tablets); (c) Take laxatives; (d) Make yourself vomit. Never = 0; occasionally = 2; once a week = 3; 2–3 times a week = 4; daily = 5; 2–3 times a day = 6; 5+ times a day = 7. Answer questions 7 (a)–(d) separately, then add them all up.	___
8. Does your pattern of eating severely disrupt your life? Yes = 1, No = 0	___
9. Would you say that food dominates your life? Yes = 1, No = 0	___
10. Do you ever eat and eat until you are stopped by physical discomfort? Yes = 1, No = 0	___
11. Are there times when all you think about is food? Yes = 1, No = 0	___

(Continued)

Table 1.1 Continued

Questions	Scores
12. Do you eat sensibly in front of others and make up in private? Yes = 1, No = 0	____
13. Can you always stop eating when you want to? Yes = 0, No = 1	____
14. Do you experience overpowering urges to eat and eat and eat? Yes = 1, No = 0	____
15. When you are feeling anxious, do you tend to eat a lot? Yes = 1, No = 0	
16. Does the thought of becoming fat terrify you? Yes = 1, No = 0	____
17. Do you ever eat large amounts of food rapidly (not a meal)? Yes = 1, No = 0	____
18. Are you ashamed of your eating habits? Yes = 1, No = 0	____
19. Do you worry that you cannot control how much you eat? Yes = 1, No = 0	____
20. Do you turn to food for comfort? Yes = 1, No = 0	____
21. Are you able to leave food on the plate at the end of a meal? Yes = 0, No = 1	____
22. Do you deceive other people about how much you eat? Yes = 1, No = 0	____
23. Does how hungry you feel determine how much you eat? Yes = 0, No = 1	____
24. Do you ever binge on large amounts of food? Yes = 1, No = 0	____
25. If yes, do such binges leave you feeling miserable? Yes = 1, No = 0	____
26. If you do binge, is this only when you are alone? Yes = 1, No = 0	____
27. If you do binge, how often is this? Hardly ever = 1; once a month = 2; once a week = 3; 2–3 times a week = 4; daily = 5; 2–3 times a day = 6	____
28. Do you go to great lengths to satisfy an urge to binge? Yes = 1, No = 0	____
29. If you overeat, do you feel very guilty? Yes = 1, No = 0	____
30. Do you ever eat in secret? Yes = 1, No = 0	____
31. Are your eating habits what you would consider to be normal? Yes = 0, No = 1	____
32. Would you consider yourself to be a compulsive eater? Yes = 1, No = 0	____
33. Does your weight fluctuate by more than 5 pounds in a week? Yes = 1, No = 0	____

Adding up and analysing the scores
Total for questions 6, 7 and 27. This will give you a severity index.   ____
Total for all other questions. This will give you a symptom score.   ____

If in addition to a problem with your eating habits you are also overweight, we suggest you include Chapter 7 in your initial reading.

Chapters 8 to 14 focus on the links between your eating disorder and the rest of your life. You can read them at a leisurely pace over the next few weeks, in whatever order you like. The aim of these additional chapters is to help you spot problems in different areas of your life, and see connections with factors that may have contributed to your eating problem or are obstacles in overcoming it.

If you drink heavily or regularly take drugs, we encourage you to look at Chapter 12 early on. Drug and alcohol problems make eating difficulties much harder to control and therefore need to be tackled early on. Chapter 12 will help you to (a) assess the seriousness of your alcohol/drug problem, and (b) decide what to do about it.

First steps

Are you ready to undertake the journey?

Read core Chapters 2, 3, 4, 5 and 6. Now. Don't try to follow any suggestions and instructions given there; skip over these for now. Re-read each chapter until you feel sure that you have been able to take the information on board. Are you ready to undertake the journey?

> • Now, when you have a quiet hour, start writing your bulimia balance sheet.
>
> First, take a large sheet of paper and divide it length-wise into two main columns. At the top of one column, write "*Reasons for giving up bulimia*", and on the other, write "*Reasons for not giving up bulimia*". You may have important reasons to fear change from familiar behaviour, and yet part of you feels desperate to escape the vicious circle that is keeping your bulimia nervosa going. Keeping all these thoughts and ideas together in your head at one time is impossible, as our memory has its limits, and so there is a tendency to swing from one side of an argument to the other. Writing a balance sheet will help you to manage your thoughts systematically. Plan to work on this for a week – keep going back to it each day.
> To focus your thoughts, make four divisions across the sheet, and at the start of each row, write:
>
> 1. Practical gains and losses for SELF
> 2. Practical gains and losses for OTHERS
> 3. Emotional gains and losses for SELF
> 4. Emotional gains and losses for OTHERS

Here, others share examples from their balance sheets to get you started. You may agree with some of the comments and want to add them to your list. But reflect and give yourself time to find your own reasons, and try to be specific. Keep this balance sheet in mind all week, as new ideas can pop up unexpectedly while you are doing something else.

Reasons to give up bulimia

1. *Practical gains for* SELF

    "I won't be tired and unwell all the time."
    "My teeth won't continue to be destroyed."
    "I will look healthier."
    "My guts will work normally without unnatural practices."
    "My body will begin to repair the damage I have caused."

2. *Practical gains for* OTHERS

    "I will be able to be with my family and friends more and will not have to make excuses to avoid eating with them."
    "My flatmates won't find the food cupboards empty."
    "I will be more romantically/sexually responsive."
    "My partner will be able to kiss me if I no longer vomit."
    "I will be less irritable and snappy."
    "I will be able to concentrate and do a better job at work."

3. *Emotional gains for* SELF

    "I won't have to lie about food and how much I eat."
    "I won't have to deceive people about vomiting and taking laxatives."
    "I will have achieved something positive."

4. *Emotional gains for* OTHERS

    "My parents will stop worrying that I will die."
    "My friends won't have to see me destroying my life."
    "At work, I will appear healthy and competent."
    "I will be able to join in all social activities without excuses."

Disadvantages of change and recovery

1. *Practical losses for* SELF

    "I will find meal-times very frightening."
    "I will feel bloated, stuffed, too full."
    "My stomach may 'blow out' after eating small amounts."
    "I may get swelling around my eyes and ankles."
    "I will become extremely anxious about my weight."

2. *Practical losses for* OTHERS

    "I will need more active help and support from my parents/partner/friend."
    "My mood may swing more."

3. *Emotional losses for* SELF

    "Letting go of my eating disorder will be so difficult that I'm bound to fail and then I will feel worse than ever."

"I will feel out of control over everything."
"I will have to face up to my responsibilities."
"I will feel uncomfortable, miserable and frightened."
"I will hate myself and my body."

4.   *Emotional losses for OTHERS*

"I may become more assertive and dominant when relieved of the burden of my eating disorder, which may upset the dynamics in my relationships."

Don't worry if distinguishing between these four categories is difficult, as there is some overlap and their role is simply to help focus your thoughts. It doesn't really matter in which category you insert your reasons, as long as they are in the correct column, that is, positive or negative.

When your balance sheet is finished, go over the list and rate each gain and loss for importance on a 1–10 scale (10 = a very important reason; 1 = only slightly important reason). Next, rate each gain and loss on a 1–10 scale for likelihood. What have you learnt from this? What are the things that might be holding you back? How likely are they to happen? What are the things that really matter to you and that might help you to start the journey?

Back to the future

We now suggest that you do the following exercise. Having your balance sheet in front of you will be helpful.

Imagine you have decided that the challenge of overcoming your eating disorder is too difficult and risky. Five years have gone by. You continue to have bulimia. Everything has gone wrong. All the negative consequences that you considered in your balance sheet have come true. You feel alone, powerless and at the end of your tether. You decide to write to your one close friend, whom you haven't seen for a while, as she (assuming your friend is a woman) has been abroad. You know that she cares about you and will not be deceived by superficial news, and that when you meet her on her return, she will see it all anyway. You have found in the past that she has been able to provide emotional and practical support when you have needed help. You know you can trust her, and must be completely open in describing your present difficulties.

Here are a few guidelines to consider in writing to your friend:

*   What weight will you be?
*   What medical complications will you have?
*   What career/job will you be pursuing?
*   Where and with whom will you be living?
*   Who will be your friends?
*   Will you be in a relationship? Married? Have children?

Now be as realistic as possible, and talk in the present tense. Here is an example of a letter from another sufferer from bulimia nervosa, who is preparing herself to undertake the journey of recovery:

Dear Susan,

I look forward to catching up when you return home in June. I thought I would tell you all about my current situation so that we can pick up where we left off when you departed five years ago. I'm afraid my story is rather sad, but I know I can trust you, and have faith that something good will come out of sharing honestly with you, as happened in the past.

My bulimia has continued, which means I have been battling it for 15 years now. My weight has fluctuated greatly, like a yo-yo, up and down, up and down. At the moment, I am on the lower end of the ideal body weight scale. I should be happy but I'm not.

I continue to vomit, although this doesn't seem as effective as it once did, and I now severely restrict my food. Preparing my food consumes my day. I keep a semblance of control by wrapping small bites in dried seaweed. In the morning, I sometimes wake to find that I have eaten at night but cannot remember it. The illness has taken a severe toll on my health. I now have six caps on my teeth, and the others remain very sensitive to temperature changes. Last summer, I was in hospital in agonizing pain with kidney stones. I had special vibration treatment to disperse them. I passed blood and gravel in my urine for weeks afterwards.

I have become more dependent on laxatives and spend all day walking to chemists' shops to buy them. I have a fixed routine and visit different shops on different days of the week. More than half my social security money goes on laxatives. The amount I need has been increasing gradually. Without them, I become so bloated and bunged up that I am terrified, and yet with them, I bleed and leak and am up all night on the toilet.

I have not worked for two years. I rent a room in a house with six others. Since David finished with me four years ago, my social life has shrunk. I only remain in contact with Sophie and Paul. They keep in touch on the phone and regularly pick me up for a visit at their house. At times, I feel so low and full of despair that I contemplate ending my suffering. I hold back as I am a coward and also because I couldn't bear to think of people seeing my room or belongings after I am dead. I would be ashamed for them to see my hoards of food (I have three freezers filled with food) and trinkets, which I have stolen from shops and never used. The compulsion to collect and clean is exhausting and overwhelming.

Despite all of this, I cling to a glimmer of hope. I remember that moment, five years ago, when you offered to help me overcome my illness. Back then, the challenge to change seemed too difficult and risky. However, I now clearly see that there is no other way forward, and I want to accept that offer of help that you so generously made before.

I know that you will be pleased that I have made this first step and have mustered the courage to write to you.

With love from Penny

- Now write your own letter to your own friend. Read it through carefully. Don't kid yourself. Be honest and open. Do you really want spend another five years shackled to your eating disorder while your friends are out having fun and getting on with life?
- Refer back to the guidelines at the start of this section. Now write a second letter. Imagine your situation in five years. This time, you have successfully overcome your bulimia because you are starting recovery work right now. Casting your mind back to the present, what steps have helped you to get well? Whose support has been invaluable? How have you managed to build momentum? What obstacles have you overcome and how? What does your future without bulimia look like? Is this the sort of future you want to aim for? That is, a future where you are the choreographer of what you do and say?

Making your decision to go

Only you can decide to work at change now or to continue with bulimia nervosa or binge eating. Probably this will not be simply one decision but numerous smaller decisions that you will make over the following days, months and years. Strong forces will try to suck you back. Expect, like others venturing on this journey, to make many mistakes. However, don't feel disheartened because *Getting Better Bite by Bite* will help you acquire skills to turn any mistake into a helpful lesson.

Asking someone to help

Trying to get better on your own is a hard and lonely task. Asking for help from family, partner or friends can be useful. Sometimes, your family, partner or friends may be more enthusiastic about helping you than you are to have them help you. If you feel unsure, read Chapter 13, as this will help you clarify whether the involvement of family members or friends in your treatment will be a positive step for you. Chapter 13 also offers guidance on how to involve others in the most helpful way, and to ascertain whether you are seeking their support for the right reasons. You will need to decide whom you will ask to give you support. Will you ask people you feel closest to or those with whom you spend the most time?

The questions outlined in Table 1.2 may help you make these important decisions.

Table 1.2 Support questionnaire

Could person X be your support? Answer the following questions:	Score
1. How easy is it to talk to X about your problem? Very easy (5 points); quite easy (4 points); not sure (3 points); quite difficult (2 points); very difficult (1 point)	___
2. Is X critical or easily upset about your eating? Always (1 point); often (2 points); sometimes (3 points); rarely (4 points); never (5 points)	___
3. Could you talk to X even if you arc not making progress? Definitely (3 points); not sure (2 points); definitely not (1 point)	___
4. Can you trust X to always be there when you need someone – with no expectations or strings attached? Definitely (5 points); probably (4 points); maybe (3 points); probably not (2 points); definitely not (1 point)	___
5. When you overcome your bulimia, what is X's response likely to be? X will feel threatened by my achievement and feel redundant (0 points) X will feel jealous of me becoming more independent and successful with my life (0 points) I haven't a clue (1 point) X will be happy for me (2 points)	___
6. How often are you in contact with X? At least once a week (3 points) At least once every two weeks (2 points) At least once a month (1 point) Less than once a month (0 points)	___
Total number of points	
Analysing your score 19 to 23 points: You are fortunate to have a perfect supporter near you. Definitely ask person X to help you in your efforts to overcome your eating disorder. 12 to 18 points: It is uncertain whether X should be your supporter. Maybe you don't know them well enough yet to be able to predict their response. Perhaps your best bet is to keep X in mind as a potential support, but not to rush into anything. However, if you do know X very well, your score may simply reflect that X is rather lukewarm about their commitment to you, and you may be better off thinking about someone else. 4 to 11 points: Look for someone else, or go it alone.	

Asking for support will be difficult. Being direct and specific about what you want your potential supporter to do is important. To help explain, we suggest you give them this book to read.

Helping someone with an eating problem is like taking on a major challenge. Some people may foresee these problems and decline to help early on. Such responses are not based on a rejection of you but the reality of their own commitments. Others may start the journey with you, wishing to please and help you without knowledge of the implications and then find it too difficult – again, expect this and know this is realism. The secondary effects of eating disorder habits lead to confusing signals to others. Sadly, there are also some people who just "don't get" bulimia and are critical and judgmental about it.

You may be fortunate to have one of those rare people around you who will be able to help and stay beside you throughout the recovery journey. The road will be difficult and treacherous for both of you, but the rewards are great. You will need to define the amount of support that will be helpful. Spend at least 15 minutes each week reviewing progress and setting new goals with your guide. You may want to show or share with your recovery guide some of the exercises we suggest in *Getting Better Bite by Bite*.

Trust is a difficult issue. The secret life of a person with an eating disorder may lead to suspiciousness in others. Discuss this with your guide. Tell them that if they become suspicious or anxious, to talk to you about their concern. Encourage them to describe the behaviour that is worrying them. They must try to be direct and present the facts, rather than be judgmental or withdraw help because of this "hump" or obstacle that appears to be blocking progress. For example, they may need to say, "*You've been working hard not to binge, and you have been able to join me for the evening meal several times this week. However, you ate very little at supper last night, appeared tense and rushed off early. I'm wondering if you've started to binge and vomit again.*"

You may work with your recovery guide to think of ways to alter your behaviour when you get an urge to eat. For example, you may come home from a difficult day at work feeling tense and hopeless, with thoughts such as "*I never do anything right*" spinning in your head. Instead of bingeing, which would temporarily suppress these thoughts, you could go for a walk with your guide, discuss together your thoughts and feelings, and return home with a fresh perspective.

Another form of support that may work for you is a self-help group, either in your neighbourhood or online. Concerned others (such as parents, partners and friends) often find these groups helpful, too. In addition, there are now resources (books[2] and DVDs[3]) for concerned others giving them unbiased information about eating disorders, helping them to manage their concerns and anxieties, and teaching them how to be supportive without being intrusive.[4]

Even if you decide to travel solo on this recovery journey, we encourage you to set aside 30 minutes each week, or more frequently, for review. Try to use your diary as a friend and confidante. Perhaps use this time to write a letter as if to a recovery guide, or draw or paint a picture or create a collage to summarise your week. End by marking goals into your diary for the coming week and evaluating what you have learned from the week before.

How to stage your journey

Before starting on *Getting Better Bite by Bite* (after browsing through it and completing the introductory exercises), you must decide – perhaps with the help of your recovery guide – to set yourself realistic and manageable goals. For instance, to state, "*I am never going to binge again in my life*" will be overwhelming and unachievable. Such an over-keen, black-and-white, unrealistic goal can make things worse instead of better by triggering more binges. Refining and breaking down your overall goals into more manageable steps is a wise way to prepare for travel. Chapters 2 to 6 provide an idea of what goals might be realistic starting points in overcoming various problematic aspects of your eating disorder. In trying to reach a goal, having an exact description of what you want to achieve is important. Describe each goal in terms of:

1.   Something that you can plan and do yourself. Be specific.
2.   Something that is measurable (not something that is impossible to measure, such as happiness).
3.   Something that challenges you slightly, so that you will feel pleased when you accomplish it, but not so difficult that even Superwoman would fail.
4.   Something defined within a realistic time frame. Having no time limit leads to procrastination. Having a goal in which you state, *"I will not do X for the rest of my life"* is unrealistic and equally unhelpful.

Get smart

The acronym SMART (specific, measurable, achievable, realistic, timeframe) summarises the features of helpful goal setting. Clear goals are the first step towards successful behaviour change.

Once you have identified your SMART goals, four other things are important:

1.   **Prioritise:** If you have identified several goals, you will need to think how best to prioritise them. Sometimes, people want to tackle all several goals at once, but as a rule of thumb, it is better to decide on one or two and really follow through with them than to do too much. Also, it might be important to start with a relatively small goal at first and try to achieve that, rather than something that is more ambitious.

2.   **Plan action:** In order to translate your goals into action, you will need to plan what will happen in what situation or at what time: how often it will happen, for how long and where it will take place (e.g. *I will add a mid-morning snack consisting of my favourite full-fat yoghurt to my diet. I will eat this around 11 a.m. after I have checked my emails at work*).

3.   **Identify obstacles:** Before starting to work on your goal(s), it will be important to identify any obstacles that could get in the way of your goal. A useful way to do this is in the form of *"if (x happens), then (I will do . . .)"* statements. Really try to visualize what could happen and then complete your *if . . . then* statements. It will be helpful to

repeat this out loud several times so that it becomes wired-in as an automatic helpful habit.

4. **Review and monitor progress towards your goal(s):** In the next chapter, you will learn about diary keeping. This can be helpful in reviewing and monitoring progress towards your goal(s).

Notes and references

1   Adapted from Henderson, M. & Freeman, C.P.L. *British Journal of Psychiatry*, 1987;150:18–24. Reproduced with permission.
2   Treasure, J., Smith, G., & Crane, A., 2007. *Skills-based learning for caregivers of a loved one with an eating disorder: The new Maudsley method.* Hove: Routledge.
3   The Succeed Foundation: http://www.succeedfoundation.org
4   Most importantly, people whose families have worked through these resources find that it makes their relationship with their family members much easier, less stressful and more supportive.

2   Tools for the journey

How to facilitate change by keeping a therapeutic diary

Take a look at the sample diary page at the back of this book. We suggest you make some copies of this page. You can then carry a single diary sheet around with you every day, and collect all the daily sheets in a folder, or you could create the page online if this is more convenient. There are also a number of commercially available eating disorder diary apps that may suit your purposes.

Alternatively, you can draw up your own diary based on the form, and in some ways, this adds to the therapeutic benefit.[1] Buy a booklet small enough to fit into your pockets or a bag. The ground rules for keeping a diary are simple:

- The diary's role is to help and support you like a best friend. Developing a friendship and trust with your diary as a safe, non-judgmental place to offload and share your thoughts is important preparation towards trusting your own self.
- For every day, write down what you eat and drink. Try to be as accurate as you can.
- Write down those occasions when you were scheduled to eat or drink, but did not do so.
- Always keep your diary with you. Take it with you even to the loo. Record even things you find shameful and embarrassing. There can be no holding back on the road to recovery.
- Record things when they are happening. In this way, you give the clearest idea of what is going on at the time.
- Do not write a novel: try to find an efficient "short-hand" way of describing what is happening at the time. Your diary is your log book on a very important journey.
- Do not leave writing your diary until you are tired and ready for bed – for greatest accuracy and benefit, note your progress several times throughout each day.

> **At the end of each week, look over your diary entries for the whole week.**
>
> What have you learnt?
> What went well and why? How can you build on this?
> What did not go so well and why? How can you reduce or prevent this from happening again?
> What are the next steps for you to take over the week to come?
> Try to be fair and compassionate to yourself in your review of the week.

Until you get into the habit of diary-keeping, you may want to break it down into stages. Get used to scribbling down and noting what you eat for a week or two; thereafter, move on to the ABC approach that we proceed to describe here. The detective work will follow.

"A" is for antecedents (triggers). **Describe in your diary:**

- Where you were at the time of eating, and what was going on (that is, were you on your own or in company, at home or at work, or elsewhere?)
- Your thoughts beforehand. Who said what?
- Your feelings beforehand.

"B" is for behaviour. **Note:**

- Whether you thought what you ate was a binge (see Chapter 4 for a definition of this).
- Whether you made yourself sick and how often.
- Whether you used laxatives or diuretics, and in what amounts.

"C" is for consequences. **Describe:**

- The consequences – both positive and negative – in both the short and long term on your thoughts, feelings and behaviour.

By answering these questions, you can create a behaviour chain:

Understanding Behavioral Chain: ABC

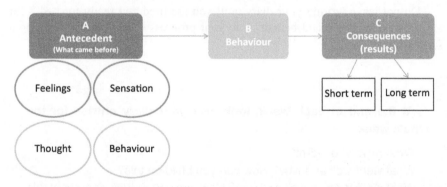

The most difficult aspect of the detective work will be to become aware of your triggering thoughts and feelings. Chapter 10, "Food for Thought", describes the thinking traps that commonly occur with eating disorders. Most triggering thoughts and feelings are unpleasant, and you may prefer not to deal with them, but the energy you use to blot them out takes a long-term toll on your well-being. Although these thoughts and feelings are not enjoyable, they are necessary and important signals that indicate you may need to change some aspects of your life. In Table 2.1, we include excerpts from a diary sheet completed by Anna, one of our patients, as an example.

Although this diary should only take a few minutes a day to complete, you are bound to find keeping it on a daily basis inconvenient at times, if not irritating. Start your diary during a week when you are not so busy that you are bound to fail to keep it.

Table 2.1 Anna's food diary, week 1 and week 4

Week 1

Time	What eaten	B	V	L	Antecedents & Consequences
8:00	All-bran				A: Still full from yesterday. C: Must make an effort not to binge today.
12:00	1 apple				A: Hungry. C: Still hungry, mustn't eat more in case it starts me off on a binge.
3:00	1 lb grapes, 2 choc. bars		!		A: Had phone call from John, he would be home late. C: Disgusted with myself. I am the most hopeless person in the world.
6:00	peanuts & chocolates, picked from shopping	!!			A: No food in flat. Had to go shopping. Couldn't stop myself putting loads of sweets in the trolley. Ate loads of stuff in the car.
		!!			Had to go on eating once at home.
7:00	2 portions of curry,	!!			C: Very angry with myself. I feel so lonely. Totally exhausted, went to bed early.
	3 choc. bars		!!		

Week 4

Time	What eaten	B	V	L	Antecedents & Consequences
8:00	Cottage cheese, 2 sl. toast with honey				Enjoyed this.
11:00	Apple				
12:30	baked potato, tuna fish				Eaten in the canteen at work. Tina said: "You haven't been here for ages." Wanted to run away; felt everybody was staring at me.
3:00	yoghurt, crunch bar				
6:00	1 sl. toast				
7:00	fish & vegetables, 1 scoop of ice cream				Had not planned dessert. John suggested ice cream. I almost said "no", but knew I would then eat all that was left in the tub while washing up. So I ate a scoop and enjoyed it while sitting with John. John put the tub away and made coffee, which we drank relaxing on the settee. Washing up left.

B = Binge, V = Vomited, L = Laxatives

We find that people vary greatly in their response to keeping this diary. You may love writing and immediately bond with your diary, able to treat it like a trusted, reliable friend in whom you love to confide. Good. You will not have any difficulties with this approach.

On the other hand, for a variety of reasons, you may find keeping a diary too difficult. You may simply find it boring. Or you may find the process of self-reflection and recording frightening and shameful and find it extremely hard to face up to what you are doing to yourself. You may be worried that someone will read your diary. Or perhaps you worry that the focus on recording all the food you eat might make you binge more instead of less. You may feel tempted to stop writing your diary every time you have had a binge. Try to be as honest as you can. Getting over this problem involves facing up to frightening feelings, thoughts and behaviour. Attempting to suppress and deny them will impede and hinder your journey to recovery.

Some people find that simply keeping a diary helps them to regularise their eating habits and facilitate progress. For others, the recovery road may not be that easy.

Shula

Shula had severe anorexia nervosa. She spent a long time in the hospital, and her weight increased to the level it had been before her illness began. However, after discharge, she began to have painful, prolonged binges. These happened every day. She induced vomiting several times a day and took about 150 laxative pills daily. She kept her food diary religiously, as she felt it provided some sense of being in control amid all her chaos. After three or four months of keeping a diary (and trying to work on her eating problem), she felt that little had changed, so why continue keeping it? Shula was asked to go over her diary again and to draw up a chart of the number of binges, episodes of vomiting, and number of laxatives taken per week (Figure 2.1).

To her surprise, she discovered that she had actually decreased all features of her eating problem, most remarkably the laxatives, but that bingeing and vomiting were also reducing gradually. You may say, "*How could she have failed to notice such a dramatic improvement?*" Well, change can be difficult to notice when drawn out over a long period of time, and especially on a bad day, when everything looks gloomy to you. Shula decided to put up the weekly chart in her bedroom to give her strength at those times when she felt she wasn't progressing.

New skills to cope with old difficulties

You will find that, in gradually learning to give up retreating into the patterns of bulimia to cope with life's difficulties, you need to develop new skills.

Learning to solve problems in seven steps

Making decisions and solving problems, small or large, is a definite skill. People vary in the ways they reach solutions for problems. Some do it just intuitively; it has to feel right emotionally or agree with certain "rules" that they live by. Others manage mainly by trying to find the most rational solution. There is no right or wrong way and we all use mixtures of these two approaches.

No. of tablets
per week

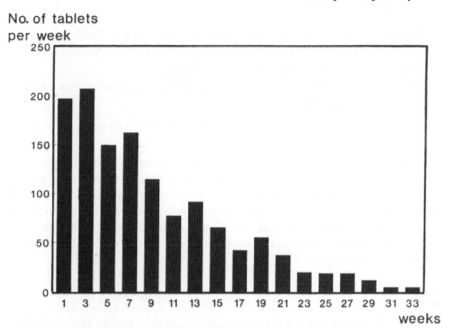

Figure 2.1 Laxative chart.

Here are seven steps that will help you find a way to take care of life's demands and stresses without defaulting to bulimia:

Step 1: What is the problem? This step may sound trivial, but you need to define your problem carefully. Write one succinct sentence to describe your problem.

Step 2: Many people get stuck because in trying to find a solution, they limit the field of possibilities. Put all constraints aside and list as many solutions as you can. Give your imagination free rein. Do not exclude anything just because it seems selfish, crazy, unrealistic or far-fetched. Jot down every solution that comes to mind.

Step 3: Look at each option in detail. List the pros and cons for each one, even for those solutions that seem silly.

Step 4: Choose a solution that fits you. Step 3 will help clarify what solution is right or wrong for you. If you still feel unsure about the best option, you may need to return to Step 2 and create more solutions, or perhaps you are not ready to address the problem you have defined. Can you shelve it for a while? What are the pros and cons of doing that?

> **Step 5**: Find ways of putting your solution into practice. Think through all the steps needed to reach your solution. Write them down.
> **Step 6:** Carry out your solution out step by step.
> **Step 7:** Check the final outcome to ensure that your solution has been a suitable one.

In Chapter 1 we showed you how to use the first steps of problem solving to make the decision to be free of bulimia or binge eating. You may want to read over your bulimia balance sheet now. As you read on in this book, you will read lots of real life examples of how people have applied problem solving to different aspects of their eating disorder. In Chapter 14, we discuss the use of problem solving in relation to career decisions. Here is an example that applies problem solving to relationships:

Andrea

> Andrea's boyfriend, Ian, had recently split up with her. Shortly afterwards, Phil, one of her old boyfriends, began to call her daily and to visit her regularly. Her parents, who had greatly disliked Ian, supported this development. Her mother would repeatedly tell her how nice Phil was, and would invite him to their house without telling Andrea. Andrea was confused and upset about splitting up with Ian, she was angry about her mother's attempts to pair her off with Phil, and she was irritated, but also flattered, by Phil's attention. She felt that the pressure she was put under, both by her mother and by Phil, to go out with him was hard to resist and that she might end up giving in to it. Moreover, the stress this caused her made her bulimia much worse. After learning about the problem-solving approach, Andrea defined her problem in terms of the seven steps:

Step 1: My problem is, I don't know what I want. Part of me knows I am not ready to enter a new relationship and that I need space and time to get over Ian, who hurt me really badly. Part of me feels that if my mother, whose judgment I trust in other things, approves of Phil, he must be good for me. And also, as he clearly cares deeply about me, maybe I'd be a fool to reject him.

Steps 2 and 3: Andrea then wrote down the following possible solutions:

(a) Become Phil's girlfriend again. Pros: This would keep everyone happy, my feeling of being under pressure would ease, I would have someone to comfort me. Cons: In the long run, I'd probably feel as discontented and bored as when I dated Phil before.

(b) Never see Phil again and ignore his phone calls and attempts at communication. Pros: This would give me space and ease pressure. Cons: I would definitely lose a good friend.

(c) Avoid my parents until they accept that I don't want to be with Phil. Pros: Again, pressure would be reduced. Cons: I would miss my parents, I like going home, and I appreciate my mother's advice on most issues.

(d) Beg Ian to make a fresh start. Pros: If he took me back, I'd be unbelievably happy. Cons: If he said "no" to me, I'd feel more rejected and hurt than I do now.

(e) Find myself another boyfriend. Pros: This would be like making a completely new start. Cons: Nice new boyfriends aren't easy to find. Moreover, at the moment, I'm not ready to feel anything for a new person.

(f) Go travelling for some months. Pros: I'd escape the misery, and the travel and new environment would help me to get over my upset. Cons: I don't have the money. Travelling can be lonely, especially when not feeling my best.

(g) Take an overdose and risk dying. Pros: This would make Ian realise how much he hurt me. Although he probably would not change his mind about finishing with me, at least I would have got back at him and taught him a lesson. Cons: I am scared of dying. I might seriously damage my health and be permanently disabled. I would feel ashamed after taking an overdose and would hurt and disappoint my parents, sisters and friends – all of whom care about me deeply.

(h) Move house and get a silent number, so that nobody can find me. Pros: This would definitely decrease hassle. Cons: I don't want to move house, and I need friends and support.

(i) Explain to my mother that, although I appreciate her opinion on many issues, on this occasion, she is wrong in trying to make up my mind for me, and explain to Phil that I do not want to be his girlfriend, but I do want to remain his friend. Pros: I would continue to get support from both my mother and Phil. I would get the space to get over Ian. Cons: Talking to my mother and Phil might be difficult, and I might hurt their feelings. My sad feelings for Ian will remain and I won't have instant relief from them.

Step 4: In considering her options more closely, Andrea realised that she didn't want to become Phil's girlfriend again, and she firmly rejected Option (a). She also rejected Options (b), (c), (e), (f), (g) and (h), which, she felt, all had an element of running away in them. This left her with two options: (d) and (i). She felt a strong pull towards being back with her old boyfriend, Ian, and therefore looked at this option in detail.

Option (d) was to beg Ian to make a new start. Pros: If he took me back, I'd be unbelievably happy. But for how long? I would continue to feel hurt over how he said he didn't want to see me anymore and would worry that he might decide to dump me a second time. Cons: If he said "no", my hurt would skyrocket. Could I cope with Ian rejecting me again?

Andrea remained unsure whether or not to take up this option. She decided to shelve it for two weeks and if, after that, she still wanted to contact Ian, she might.

She then considered Option (i). She thought: There is nothing to stop me from getting on with that now. Whatever happens with Ian, I need to sort things out with my mother and Phil.

Steps 5 and 6: Andrea decided to approach Phil first, which, she knew, would be easier. She told him that she appreciated his friendship and would always do so, but that she felt he was looking for more than that from her. She said she did not want to become his girlfriend again, especially as she still felt very upset about Ian.

Andrea knew that talking to her mother would be difficult, so, in preparation, she jotted down on notepaper what she wanted to say: "Mum, I need to talk to you about something that is bothering me. You know I am still pretty upset about Ian, and you have been a great help with listening to me so patiently. But there is one thing that is not helping. You keep inviting Phil a round to cheer me up, but it just doesn't work. You would help me more if you stopped doing that." She considered how her mother might react to this. There was some risk that her mother would get upset and cross. Andrea thought that choosing a good time to discuss the issue would be crucial and that, even if her mother did get upset, she would not hold it against her for the rest of her life.

She waited until she and her mother were alone at home, relaxing on a Saturday afternoon. Then she made her approach. As she predicted, her mother was upset. She said that she had only wanted to help, that Andrea was accusing her of match-making, which she had never tried to do, and that in the future, she would leave Andrea to sort out her own problems. Andrea left her mother feeling shaken up but convinced that she had done the right thing.

Step 7: Andrea's mother did stop inviting Phil around and making references to him, and two weeks later, she apologised to her daughter for having tried to interfere in her life. Phil continued to call Andrea frequently, but somehow their conversation had cleared the air, and she no longer felt pressured by his phone calls. The reduction in stress and pressure also eased Andrea's binge eating somewhat, and the fact that she had successfully dealt with her relationship difficulty gave her more confidence to make further changes to tackle her bulimia.

Andrea's example shows that often, big complicated problems can be broken down into smaller ones that can be tackled separately and that sometimes giving yourself permission to shelve aspects of a problem can be helpful, too. It also shows there is not necessarily a neat solution to a problem and that, like Andrea, in choosing an option, you may choose some risks and problems, too.

Note and reference

1   The therapeutic benefits of diary keeping are based on what is called "self-monitoring". Centrally, this involves noticing and measuring certain symptoms (including thoughts, feelings, physical sensations and behaviours) and becoming aware of factors (both internal [such as feelings] and external [such as certain environments or interactions with people]) that start certain behaviours, or make them better or worse. But this is not meant to be a dry exercise in "accountancy". Rather, the thing that makes self-monitoring helpful is if you can use it as a tool for learning about yourself and also as a tool for setting, reviewing and monitoring your goals.

Knowing your patterns of behaviour and what drives them is the start of successful planning for change. An important part of self-monitoring is "affect labelling". Putting a label on and describing to yourself what you feel (including what mixture of feelings/emotions you have) and how intense your feelings are can be helpful in taking the heat out of them and give them less power. The reason for this is that by verbalizing our emotional response, we activate parts of the brain that dampen down our limbic system (an old part of the brain involved in generating emotions) (Craske, M.G., Treanor, M., Conway, C.C., Zbozinek, T., Vervliet, B. Maximizing exposure therapy: an inhibitory learning approach. *Behaviour Research and Therapy*, 2014 Jul;58:10–23.).

3 Dieting

A health warning

Beauty is in the eye of the beholder

What constitutes the ideal body shape has varied throughout history and will continue to do so. Fashion trends thrive on change and people's desire to "fit in" and conform. The preferred female or male body shape in five years from now is anybody's guess, but we know one thing for sure – very few people will naturally fit whatever shape is "in".

Rosamund

Rosamund, at 17 a promising ballerina, was told by her principal that her technique and presentation were excellent, but that she had a problem – her breasts were several sizes too big. Plastic surgery was recommended as a solution. This upset Rosamund deeply. She eventually wanted to marry and have children. Rather than risk interference with this yearning by having an operation for the sake of her art, Rosamund decided a diet was her only option. She restricted her food intake severely, but bulimia quickly developed, and her weight increased rather than fell.

Men as well as women are vulnerable to developing an eating disorder when under pressure to take drastic measures to conform to an unnatural body shape or weight.

Stephen

Stephen, a builder, lost a foot in a car accident. He became interested in health and fitness and went to the gym to train regularly. Friends there suggested that he use steroids to build up his muscles. He did, but his family and girlfriend became concerned about the change in his personality. He became more irritable and lost his temper at the slightest provocation. One day, while driving, he became enraged when overtaken by another car. He set off in pursuit, despite his girlfriend's protests. She died in the resulting car crash.

Men taking anabolic steroids have been known to commit serious crimes, including murder. The dangers, sacrifices and mutilations to which people submit themselves for the sake of some ideal or perception of beauty are both shocking and astounding. Perhaps the answer has something to do with human nature. With the loss of beliefs in gods and fate, the whims and chances of nature are increasingly considered to be under personal control. No longer do we say, "she has all the luck", "the gods smiled on her". Any deviation from normality is blamed upon mistakes, neglect and poor lifestyle. The myth is that you, too, can be beautiful if you try hard enough or spend enough money and time on potions, diets, exercise and surgery.

In the healthy weight range

Table 3.1 gives the weight ranges (for different heights) into which most people fall. As with height and shoe size, a large range of weights is considered normal and healthy. Some people are heavier than others, just as some people have bigger feet. (The current fashion of slimness is on a par with the ancient fashion in China for women to have small feet. Instead of crippling bandages, we now have diet "straitjackets".) Both practices have had a severe impact on health and lifestyle. Extreme overweight and underweight is associated with ill health and a shorter life.

If your weight is above the weight band given for your height, we suggest you look at Chapter 7, which has been written especially for you.

Table 3.1 The weight band that is appropriate for your height

Height (ft/ins)	Height (metres)	Weight (lbs)	Weight (kg)
5' 0"	1.50	100 to 124	45–56
5' 1"	1.52	102 to 128	46–58
5' 2"	1.56	106 to 133	48–60
5' 3"	1.58	109 to 135	49–61
5' 4"	1.61	113 to 141	51–64
5' 5"	1.63	114 to 143	52–65
5' 6"	1.66	119 to 150	54–68
5' 7"	1.68	124 to 153	56–69
5' 8"	1.70	128 to 159	58–72
5' 9"	1.73	133 to 165	60–75
5' 10"	1.75	135 to 170	61–77
5' 11"	1.77	140 to 175	63–79
6' 0"	1.80	141 to 177	65–81

What weight is right for me?

Your weight and shape is determined mainly by your physical constitution. The genes that you inherited, and that programme your body, cannot be changed. To assess the weight and shape you may have inherited:

> - Draw your family tree in your diary, and write in the weights and heights of your family members.
> - Collect photographs of your grandmothers, grandfathers, great-aunts, mother, father, aunts and uncles when they were your age. Paste them in an album.

Enid

Enid came from a plump family; her mother, aunt and grandmother had all been stout. She developed early and was bigger than all her school friends. She was ashamed when her periods began while she was at junior school. She started to diet when she read on the back of a packet of tights that her ideal weight was 30 lbs below her current weight. She never reached that weight because bulimia began.

If, like Enid, you come from a family in which most members are plump, it is likely that your healthy weight will be at the top end of the normal range.

Muscles and bones are much denser than fat tissue. If you are an athlete, or the rest of your family have an athletic build, you should also expect your weight to be at the top end of the normal range. Similarly, if everyone in your family is big-boned, you, too, are likely to be at the top end of the normal range.

For many sufferers of bulimia, achieving a healthy weight simply means going back to the weight they were before their eating problems began. For some of you, this message will be hard to swallow.

Are weight fluctuations normal?

A person's weight normally goes up and down over time by about 4 to 5 lbs (2 kg) or more. If your weight goes up 5 lbs one day, it does not follow that it will continue to do this.

Rapid weight changes are not normal but do occur as part of bulimia due to fluid shifts (Chapter 5). Therefore, daily checking of weight[1] is pointless as a control measure. Moreover, it is likely to make you much more anxious.

- Be bold: give your scales away, throw them away, or at least put them in a place where you can't reach them easily (the loft or the cellar).
- Or, if you aren't brave enough to do that, draw up a timetable and a plan to gradually reduce the number of times you weigh yourself. Aim to weigh yourself no more than once a week.

Is weight the only important indicator of health?

No. Research shows that the ratio of waist measurement to hip measurement is a better predictor of health than weight. Waist size divided by hip size should be less than 0.9, that is, your waist should be less than nine-tenths of your hip size. The traditional pear shape of women, although currently devalued, is a shape associated with health and a low risk of illness.

Cavemen did not eat ice-cream

Evolution and our genes have not caught up with two changes in our environment to which we need to adapt: (1) most of us have little or no exercise and sit most of the day, and (2) our diet contains foods prepared to be highly palatable usually with a high degree of fat and high levels of refined sugars. These foods that hit the "spot" are marketed as delicious, affordable and accessible.

Diets don't work

The greatest pressure to lose weight is on those members of our society who have a natural tendency to being overweight. However, dieting is not the answer because as a rule of thumb, DIETS DO NOT WORK. Yes, they may lead to weight loss

in the short term, but the more rigid, extreme and monotonous the weight-loss regime, the less sustainable it is, meaning that in the longer term, most people who go on such weight loss diets regain everything they lost and more. And, of course, such diets are also a powerful trigger for bingeing.

> • Go online or to your local bookshop and see how many articles, books and magazines there are on slimming and diets. How can there be such a big market for these items? Why are new diets and diet books constantly promoted in the media? The answer is, of course, that they do not work. Slimming is marketed as any other hobby, but unfortunately, it will not only take your money and absorb you, but also put your health at risk and possibly entrap you for life.

Doctors are affected by the propaganda, too, and some may suggest a lower weight may be healthy for you.

Georgina

Georgina went to her general practitioner with a problem with her feet. He weighed her and said that she was overweight. She began to diet and lose weight, but soon she developed bulimia. Twenty years later, she presented to a specialised clinic; her teeth were destroyed, and surgeons were advising her to have her large intestine removed to remedy chronic constipation and stomach pain caused by her chronic abuse of laxatives.

Health hazards of dieting

Many large-scale studies show that people whose weight has fluctuated often or greatly – that is, who have gone on many diets – have a higher risk of dying from heart disease. In fact, the risk of early death may be as high in people who diet a lot as in those who are massively obese.

Dieting is dangerous

Weight loss has profound effects on both physical and psychological health.

Effects of starvation on the body

1. Sensitivity to cold: this includes cold extremities, which may lead to chilblains.
2. Sleep disturbances: waking up early or several times in the night.
3. Weak bladder: passing water frequently throughout the day or night.
4. Excess hair growth on the body.
5. Poor circulation, slow pulse and fainting spells.
6. Thin bones: with time, this may result in fractures, leading to pain and deformity.
7. Periods stop or become very irregular. A woman usually can have periods only when 15% of her body is composed of fat.
8. The stomach shrinks and feels uncomfortably distended after eating even a small amount of food.
9. Gut function is decreased, and constipation results.
10. The bone marrow, where the red and white cells in the blood are formed, is sluggish, which can result in anaemia.
11. Lack of nourishment damages the liver so that it is unable to manufacture body proteins. This may cause swelling in the ankles and legs.
12. Blood cholesterol level is increased. This results from the lack of oestrogen (before menopause, oestrogen protects women from heart attacks) and because of abnormal liver function.
13. General tiredness may lead to muscular weakness and paralysis.
14. In young girls, growth may be stunted and puberty delayed.

Effects of starvation upon the mind

1. Mood is lowered, with tearfulness and pessimism.
2. The mind becomes preoccupied with food, and there is often a strong urge to overeat.

3.   Ability and interest in forming relationships is diminished.
4.   Concentration is poor, and it is difficult to function fully.
5.   Minor problems appear insurmountable.
6.   Complex thought is impaired.

These lists are dry and dull, but many authors have written about the effects of starvation on human thinking and behaviour.

You may say, *"I did lose weight when I got concerned about my size, but since then, I have put on weight. So can the problems described here still apply to me?"* The answer is *"yes"*, definitely, as a common pattern is to alternate fasting with bingeing. If you don't eat for more than four hours, your body starts to enter starvation mode and switches all the metabolic processes to those that conserve energy.

How much do I need to eat?

Appetite is tightly linked to energy expenditure. This is known as metabolic rate. Your body has to work harder and needs more energy when you exercise or if you are in a cold climate. Hormonal changes in our body also affect metabolism. Women in the second half of their menstrual cycles are metabolically more active as their bodies prepare themselves for egg implantation. One sign of this increased metabolism is the increase in body temperature seen after ovulation. You may have been aware of your increased appetite pre-menstrually and felt frightened by it.

There are no easy rules. People differ in the amount of energy they need, and all the factors mentioned here affect and alter your energy requirements. As soon as you reduce your food intake, your body will clamp down on its energy expenditure, and losing weight will be more difficult. Your body will do this more quickly and more efficiently the more times you try to diet. This has been called weight cycling.

You need to eat 1800 to 2000 calories per day if you are a young adult female and mainly sedentary but if your levels of activity are high or you are still growing or you are male, you will need considerably more. However, we suggest that rather than count calories for your meals, choose portion sizes similar to those that other people eat, or that are available to be bought.

Achieving optimal weight and shape

Long gaps between meals switch the body into storage mode, and nutrients are selectively deposited in storage depots on the expectation of famine. When the balance between fat and lean body tissue is disturbed, weight may increase to keep the amount of lean tissue constant. Eating only at night has a similar effect. At this time, the body's hormones prepare for the fast during sleep and promote storage of energy into fat deposits.

Imelda

Imelda came to London from Northern Ireland to marry her boyfriend. She quickly had a baby and keeping in touch with her old work colleagues had been difficult. Her husband's friends were not very welcoming towards her, and she felt lonely and isolated. With her family in Northern Ireland, she had nobody she could turn to for help. Her eating became chaotic. Each morning, she would wake up and vow to eat nothing and, indeed, she would eat no meals. However, when she came home after finishing her shopping, having eaten nothing all day, the prospect of coping with the chaos of her lively son playing in the small sitting room led her to eat six or seven bags of crisps, followed by a chocolate bar. To make up for this, she would redouble her efforts to avoid meals the next day. All the time, her weight increased steadily.

To work with your body, you need to:
- Eat the majority of your food before evening. If you can, have your main meal at lunchtime.
- Eat small amounts regularly throughout the day. (Thus, in addition to 3 meals, have 2–3 snacks. Protein-rich snacks in particular are helpful in staving off feelings of hunger.)
- Exercise regularly, though not excessively.
- Restrict your consumption of fat but ensure that protein and carbohydrates are adequate.
- Avoid multiple courses, as they are likely to make you overly full.

Making a start

The first step to get your eating under control is to ensure that you are eating regularly throughout the day. You may say, "*If I start eating in the morning, then I will binge all day.*" Yes, you are right, there may be a brief phase when you fear you will be unable to stop eating after a meal, so prepare for this and be extra vigilant. You will need to have an alternate "*if . . . then*" plan in mind, which you rehearse out loud: "*If my fullness signals do not switch on, then I will leave the house to go for a walk/go to my pleasant activity box*" *etc.* (A pleasant activity box should be a collection of reminders or tools to capture your attention until your new learning about food signals kicks in. For example: sort my photo collection, Facebook or email friend, tidy a drawer, do some DIY etc.)

This is a good time to ask for extra support from your recovery guide – explain you need help to get through this difficult but very important part of your journey. The goal of regular meals throughout the day is essential.

Do not try to lose weight at this stage. If you do, the vicious circles of bulimia will just go on and on. You may say, "*I can't give up trying to lose weight. It is too important.*" Yes, letting go of something that is important to you is challenging and tough. Perhaps it is easiest if you just persuade yourself to put losing weight on hold for a while (a day, a week, a month, six months at a time). This way, it will be less frightening.

Also, once your eating pattern becomes less chaotic, your weight may decrease naturally, or the balance between fat and lean tissue may improve.

Plan A: For those without any pattern to their eating

If your eating pattern is totally chaotic, aim to re-introduce regular meals one by one. For example, can you manage a baked potato with cottage cheese for lunch? Do not be too ambitious, and do be honest with yourself. Choose something you feel safe in eating, preferably with safeguards to end the meal. Discuss this with your recovery guide and seek their support. Can you promise to eat this item every day? Expect this stage to be two steps forward and one back. Keep persisting. Every normal meal you eat is a small victory.

*   Draw up a list of 10 small meals that you think would be easiest for you to attempt to eat.
*   Rank them in order of difficulty, with the most difficult at the bottom.
*   Start with the meal at the top of the list.
*   Plan to eat that meal at some time in the day before 3 p.m.

How can you ensure that this meal will not lead to a binge? Let's consider some strategies. Ask yourself:

*   Can I eat this meal with someone else?
*   Can I eat this meal in a canteen or cafe?
*   Can I arrange to do something I enjoy for half an hour immediately after my meal?

Your anxiety and guilt levels before, during and after this meal will be high. Perhaps there will be additional difficult emotions, too. To deal with these emotions:

*   Keep a notebook and pencil beside you. Name and write down the emotion or blend of emotions you are experiencing.[2] Draw a vertical line (or several if you are experiencing different emotions) and mark it/them 0–10 (0 = no emotion [e.g. anxiety]; 10 = very intense emotion [e.g. utter panic or overwhelming guilt])
*   Put a mark where your anxiety/guilt level is now.
*   Every five minutes, mark your level of anxiety/guilt while eating and for two hours after eating. Your recovery guide may be able to help you with this recording.

- What exactly are the thoughts going through your mind now that you are leading to these emotions? These thoughts may be vague and jumbled – that doesn't matter. Jot them down, even if they seem incomplete, frightening or silly.
- Try to keep adding to the list over the next few hours.
- The next day, when you eat another meal, take out your book and repeat this process – and so on, every day.
- Later, when you are relaxed, take out your notebook and re-read the thoughts that you have written.
- Show them to your recovery guide, or imagine showing them to a close and compassionate friend.
- What would they say about your thoughts about food?
- Get them to read this chapter. What do they say now about your thoughts?
- Record exactly what they say in your notebook.
- At the end of their replies to each of your list of thoughts about eating, indicate on a scale of 0 to 10 your level of agreement with their comment.
- Repeat this process each day.
- Try to catch any new thoughts you may have when faced with food.
- Try to make up your own replies to these new thoughts.
- Keep eating exactly the same meal each day with the same routine until your anxiety level at the beginning of the meal has fallen by at least 2 points. Then you may be ready to try to eat the next item on your list.
- With the next meal, go through exactly the same procedure as before. Once you have been able to manage two different meals, try to eat two meals before 3 p.m. each day. Go through exactly the same procedure as before. The next stage, thereafter, will be to eat two meals and a snack before 3 p.m. each day. Do not worry if your diet is rather monotonous at the moment.[3]

Plan B: For those with some degree of order to their eating

If your eating pattern is reasonably regular, what is the size of your meal? Are you eating sufficient calories early in the day?

- Gradually plan to shift your eating so that more calories are eaten earlier in the day. Aim to eat 30% at breakfast and 40% for lunch.

Regaining eating control

- Try to eat in a room or pleasant space that is separate from where food is stored and prepared. Eat all your meals in this place.
- Make every meal look as appetizing and attractive as possible.
- Lay out a table-cloth or place-mat and serviette.
- Make your place setting as attractive as possible.
- Bring your plate in from a different room, leaving behind all the food containers in the other room.

- Don't distract yourself with television, radio or reading. This 15 minutes is set aside to relearn about food.
- Look at your plate for 30 seconds before starting to eat. Put down your knife and fork between each mouthful. What does the plate look like now? Make sure you know how the food tastes and feels in your mouth. Chew carefully and take longer before you swallow.

What should I eat and when?

Your ultimate target is three meals almost equally divided in calorie numbers and each well balanced for protein (for example, cheese, eggs, meat, fish, beans) and carbohydrates (e.g. bread, pasta, potatoes, rice), with a small snack between each meal.

Remember these tips:

- Protein is more satisfying, calorie-for-calorie, than other food items.
- Hot food is more satisfying than cold food.
- Solid food is more satisfying than liquid food.

Ensure that there is no gap longer than three hours without a small snack, e.g. a drink and some fruit.

Table 3.2 shows the diet plan of Thelma, who had gained weight with bulimia. She was pleasantly surprised to find she lost weight following this plan.

Table 3.2 Thelma's diet plan

Time	Meal	What eaten
8:15	Breakfast	Fruit juice, 1 individual box of cereal, 200 ml skimmed milk, 1 slice of brown bread, 1 pat margarine, 1 spoon marmalade, 1 pot of tea or coffee
10:30	Mid-morning snack	Coffee with milk (skimmed), 1 piece of fruit
12:30	Lunch	Main course: piece of grilled meat with rice and salad or vegetarian dish
Pudding: yoghurt, fruit salad or fruit, 1 cup of tea/coffee
3:30	Mid-afternoon snack	Tea with skimmed milk, piece of fruit or yoghurt or 2 plain savoury biscuits
6:30	Supper	Main course: same as lunch – fruit/yoghurt, 1 cup of water, 1 cup of tea with skimmed milk
	Bedtime	Hot drink with skimmed milk

- It may be easier if you follow exactly the same diet each day and gradually make exchanges so that the variety of your food is gradually increased, e.g. fish rather than chicken, or a pear for a snack rather than an apple.
- Be wise: travel like the tortoise. Changing long-standing habits is difficult, but definitely doable.

How can I judge what amount to eat?

You are right. Deciding "how much is enough" is hard to work out. Some solutions:

- Eat with other people, and choose the same-sized portions as them.
- Buy individual meals (frozen or long-life).
- Avoid artificial sweeteners. These feed misinformation into your body. The artificial sweetener tricks your body and undoes years of learning about the metabolic consequences of food. Your body will learn: sweetness = no or little energy. Your body's instincts therefore will drive you to eat large quantities of sweet things as it strives for adequate nourishment.

How to end your meals

There are many signals that the body uses to finish eating. All of these get upset with bulimia and binge eating.

1. How a meal looks: all living creatures learn to predict how much energy and nutrients they will later absorb from a given food just by the look of it.
2. The taste and smell of foods are clues that remind our body what effect a given food will have on our blood sugar.
3. The feeling of fullness in our stomach is another sign to indicate that we have had sufficient nutrition.
4. Finally, hunger is satisfied for several hours by the nutrients that are absorbed into the blood.

As these normal ways of ending meals have been disturbed with bulimia, you may initially need to make triggers to end a meal.

Susan

Susan knew that whenever, and whatever, she ate, she would end up binge-ing. She also could eat nothing in the presence of others, though she was able to confide in others and ask them to help. To create an end-of-meal trigger, she asked her friend to knock on her door 15 minutes after starting a meal, go with her to put her food away, take her locker key, and sit and chat over coffee with her for an hour.

Alternatively, you may choose a specific food to signal the end of a meal.

Katie

Katie lived alone in a flat, and devised a plan of eating a plain grapefruit at the end of each meal. The ritual of peeling, and then the sharp, bitter taste, was a powerful ending signal.

You will be able to think of many other ways to successfully trigger completion of your meal and divert your attention away from food until the time for your next snack or meal.

Notes and references

1   Weighing yourself daily or even multiple times a day can be thought of as a "safety behaviour", i.e. a behaviour designed to reduce your fears (e.g. of out-of-control weight gain) and thus make you feel better in the short term. However, experts have discovered that such safety behaviours in the longer term keep the person stuck with their problems and inhibit new learning, such as having experiences that disconfirm deeply held (unhelpful) beliefs (Craske, M.G., Treanor, M., Conway, C.C., Zbozinek, T., Vervliet, B. *Behaviour Research and Therapy*, 2014 Jul;58:10–23).

2   We have already described in Chapter 2, Note 1, the technique of affect labelling and here we are asking you to use it again. Putting a label on and describing to yourself what you feel (including what mixture of feelings/emotions you have) and how intense your feelings are can be helpful in taking the heat out of them and give them less power. The reason for this is that by verbalizing our emotional response, we activate parts of the brain that dampen down our limbic system (an old part of the brain involved in generating emotions) (Craske, M.G., Treanor, M., Conway, C.C., Zbozinek, T., Vervliet, B. *Behaviour Research and Therapy*, 2014 Jul;58:10–23).

3   Ultimately, we do want you to be able to eat a variety of foods with different calorie contents. But it is better to start with manageable goals and then to move to more ambitious goals over time.

4 The black hole of the insatiable stomach

The definition of "bulimia" is "eating like an ox". Most people with a bulimic disorder describe binges as the central and most unpleasant aspect of their eating difficulties.

Andrew, a 22-year-old student, describes his binges:

> *Once I start, I stuff myself until completely full and bloated. I worry some-times that my stomach might burst. I can hardly breathe. I eat very quickly,*

and barely notice what I put into my mouth. I don't chew the food. The worst thing is this feeling of being totally out of control, of having to go on eating; it takes me over. I cannot stop until I'm absolutely stuffed.

People vary greatly in the kinds of food they eat during a binge and in the amount consumed. We define a binge as any large amount of food that is eaten rapidly and with loss of self-control. Occasional overeating is part of many people's lives and is not unhealthy.

Other people don't exactly binge, but follow a somewhat different pattern of overeating – so-called grazing or compulsive overeating, that is, instead of eating a lot all at once, they nibble all day without being able to stop.

Sonya

Sonya had a very difficult childhood, with her parents getting divorced when she was six. Thereafter, her mother had a seemingly endless stream of boyfriends. Sonya: *"When a new man was on the scene, my mother hardly noticed me. They would be out together most nights of the week. She'd give me lots of pocket-money though, to keep me quiet. After a while, things would go wrong, and there would be arguments, sometimes physical fights. Then the boyfriend would get kicked out, and I would be left with a mother who was miserable and bad-tempered, who withdrew to her bedroom for days. I had nothing to turn to but food. I would sit there day in, day out, eating one biscuit or sweet after another, to make that horrible loneliness go away. By the age of 13, I weighed 168 lbs, although I am only 5 ft tall. At school, nobody wanted to be my friend. So I ate more."*

Even though now in a stable relationship with a supportive partner, Sonya overeats when he isn't around: *"My partner often goes on business trips and may be away for several days at a time. When alone in the house, I eat all day, slowly and steadily, like I constantly have to keep my hands and mouth busy. Sometimes I think this stems from flashbacks of the old feeling of having nobody who cares. At other times, I haven't a clue why I just nibble all day."*

In this chapter, we focus our discussion mainly on bingeing; however, if you graze, nibble, comfort-eat or compulsively overeat, these descriptions of the mechanisms involved will be helpful for you, too.

Most people binge/graze/comfort-eat on high-calorie foods, which may be sweet or savoury. Some people overeat on food that they secretly love but see as "unhealthy" or "forbidden" and therefore only eat during a binge. Others eat whatever comes their way, even food they don't like. Some people go as far as eating frozen food or scavenging through rubbish bins to find something to eat. The experience of overeating regularly is highly demoralising and makes most people feel that they have failed abysmally.

Why can't I control my eating?

Bingeing is not the result of being a weak-willed person. There are a number of important biological and psychological reasons for bingeing.

Biological reasons

Bingeing can be the direct result of starvation. By giving you strong cravings for food, your body will tell you loud and clear that it is not getting enough nutrition. These cravings can be constant or intermittent. The harder you try to reduce your food intake, the more you will be prone to bingeing. Often people make things worse by cutting out meals after a binge to compensate for having eaten so much. Unfortunately, instead of helping, this meal avoidance behaviour automatically programmes the next binge. In addition, alcohol and drugs, which reduce inhibitions, may make you binge more.

As explained below, alternating between starving and bingeing can also link to addiction-like changes in the brain, "wanting becomes wired in", which make it harder for people to stop bingeing once the pattern has been well established.

Psychological reasons

Boredom, depression, stress, tension and loneliness often lead to bingeing because food, at least at the start of a binge, is comforting and eases these negative feelings. Sometimes a small slip from a rigid and inadequate diet may make you so demoralised that you decide to give up control completely and have a binge.

Physiological and psychological reasons for bingeing are not mutually exclusive and often occur in the same person at the same time.

How to stop binges

Many people feel that if only their binges could be cured, they wouldn't have a problem. Unfortunately, bingeing as a symptom can't be treated in isolation. To overcome the physiological aspects of bingeing, you need to:

- work on eating regularly at meal-times (see Chapter 2) to give your body proper nutrition and thereby to reduce strong cravings for food that are going to set you off again.
- try as hard to keep to a normal meal pattern after bingeing, as missing a meal will programme the next binge.
- deal with the consequences of bingeing, that is, vomiting (see Chapter 5).

By addressing these aspects of your problem, you soon will find that binges decrease in duration and frequency.

Am I addicted to food?

For many sufferers of bulimia, cravings for food, and often especially sweet food, can be so powerful that it feels like an addiction. You also may have the experience that, as soon as you eat something sweet, you need more and more, reinforcing your sense of powerlessness vis-à-vis sweets. Sugary foods enter our bloodstream more quickly than other foods. This increase in blood sugar leads to release of the insulin hormone. This in turn facilitates the uptake of sugar into body cells, causing a drop in blood sugar level. Low blood sugar leads to the desire to eat more sweet things. This effect is particularly marked if you are undernourished. Also, if you drink large amounts of artificially sweetened diet drinks, your body learns to associate the pleasant taste of sweetness with little nutritional value and will drive you to eat large amounts.

Some sweet foods, like chocolate, lead to the release of endorphins, morphine-like "happy-making" substances produced by the brain, making this type of sweet seem very rewarding to eat.

Over the past 10 years or so, we have learnt a lot about food addiction from research in small laboratory animals. If, instead of feeding these animals with a somewhat boring but healthy diet of chow, they are given time-limited access (e.g. for an hour a day) to pure sugar or highly sugary biscuits, they will start eating increasingly large amounts during their limited period of access to this food in a manner that strongly resembles human binge-eating. If the animal's stomach content gets emptied out by putting a tube in their stomach (resembling what happens during vomiting), they will binge even more. If this experiment is kept up over a period of time, it can be shown by looking at the brains of these animals that they show addiction-like brain changes. Moreover, if these food-addicted animals are given access to other potentially addictive substances like alcohol, they become addicted to that much more readily than animals that are not food-addicted.

Neuroimaging studies in people also confirm that there are addiction-like changes in brains of people who have bulimia or binge-eat regularly. Another important finding from animal studies is that animals vary hugely in the extent to which they are "binge-prone". However, even animals that are not binge-prone to start with can be made to become binge-prone if they are first subjected to stress and then exposed to short periods of sugary food and long periods of no food. The take home message here is that, given certain circumstances (stress, combined with a pattern of starving, bingeing and purging), pretty much anyone can become locked into a problem that feels compulsive and out of control.

You will find that by following our advice in Chapter 3 and working on eating more normally, the "wired in" wanting that underpins your feeling of being addicted to food will lessen and eventually disappear, so there is no need to give up sweet foods altogether. However, new learning takes time and practice, practice, practice (maybe 5,000 hours). This involves practising new helpful habits in multiple situations and environments.[1]

While your eating pattern is chaotic, monitor your intake of sweets carefully and eat them only in conjunction with other foods (to avoid low blood sugar after eating the sweet). When you have a little more control over your eating, you might like to set yourself the task of eating a small amount of chocolate or cake every day, to prove to yourself that you can enjoy "danger" foods without triggering a binge.

Addressing the psychological aspects of bingeing

You need to become aware of your own triggers, which are influenced by your body and mind. Your diary will help with this (see Chapter 1). Here are some examples from former sufferers:

Anna

Anna, 23, had a long journey to work, with the route requiring several bus changes. "*Each time I got off a bus, I would walk past a sweet shop and buy something to eat.*" Because Anna knew that she would binge on her journey to work, she didn't allow herself any breakfast.

To counter this trigger, Anna decided to eat a regular breakfast before leaving for work. She also realised that checking her work emails on her smart phone on her journey to work, as she often did, made her anxious and stressed and was not a good start to the day. As her journey required several changes, reading a book was not really possible. Using the problem-solving approach described in Chapter 2, Anna came up with several potential solutions, including looking at different routes (to avoid sweetshops) and using different modes of transport to work, but all of these had some drawbacks. The solution she chose was to listen to her favourite music or an audiobook or mindfulness work out on her journey to work. These simple measures were a great help in reducing her bingeing episodes.

Belinda

Belinda started work at lunch-time. Mornings were an unstructured time. There was nobody to have breakfast with, as she liked to get up late after her mother had left the house. Sometimes Belinda would exercise in the morning, which she didn't enjoy but felt was good for her. However, when feeling tired after a late night, she could not motivate herself to exercise, and would have a binge instead. Belinda's solution was to do something she liked before work that would get her out of the house. She arranged to attend acting lessons in the morning, and made sure she had time for breakfast before going out. As a result, her bingeing rate reduced.

Ros

When Ros came to our clinic, she binged four to six times a week. Binges could happen at any time during the day, in different places. There did not seem to be a particular pattern. She felt very out of control and couldn't say what triggered her binges. She was asked to put into her diary details of everything that happened from the moment she first had the thought of bingeing to the moment when she actually binged.

It became clear that very often before an actual binge, there was a build-up of several hours during which small things would go wrong and the voice in her head saying, "*Go on, have a binge*" would get "*louder*" and more seductive and more difficult to resist. This would lead to increased food craving, tension and frustration and often result in a binge. On one day, for example, she had nothing to do at work. At 2 p.m., she thought of bingeing for the first time. She rejected the thought firmly and distracted herself with a computer game. By 4 p.m., she had nothing to distract her, and the thought of bingeing came back. A friend then rang and cancelled their evening outing. At that point, Ros went to the bank and withdrew money to buy food for her binge. She tried to call another friend to go out but was turned down. By now, she was so upset that she went home and binged.

Over a period of time, Ros became very good at identifying "danger" situations. She realised that she had used bingeing as an easy solution to suppress many minor irritations in her life. For each "danger" situation, she learnt a more appropriate way of dealing with it. For example, feeling bored and unfulfilled at work was a recurring problem (she was a receptionist, and there were long stretches of sitting about, doing nothing).

Ros began using slack times at work to do some reading towards a part-time degree course, and no longer felt she had wasted the whole day. She decided that if friends let her down for evening arrangements, she would go to the cinema on her own instead, rather than sit at home and mope, which would invariably lead to a binge. She also used the image of a small gremlin that was trying to persuade her to binge *("Go on, it would be lovely to have some cream cake now!")* in order to describe and visualize her unhelpful thoughts and preoccupations with food. Using the image of the gremlin helped her to be more aware of these permission-giving thoughts and fight back, before they became so elaborate and enticing that they were too hard to resist.

Karen's story illustrates that even if you understand the psychological reasons for your binges, it may not always be easy to give them up very quickly, especially if there is a strong element of comfort.

Karen

Karen was a single working mother in her thirties. She had been sexually abused as a child. When she first came to see us, she binged and vomited several times a day. She then learnt to eat more during the day, and as a result, reduced bingeing and vomiting to once at night, which she was very pleased about. She kept saying she wanted to improve more and give up bingeing and vomiting altogether, but somehow she couldn't. After a lot of discussion about why she had got so stuck at this point, it turned out that she felt her life was a constant struggle. She greatly missed having a partner who cared for her, but at the same time, she was extremely frightened of entering a relationship with a man, given her traumatic childhood experience. She identified that bingeing was the only thing in her life that was easy, pleasurable and comforting, and made her lonely evenings more bearable.

These examples show that there are many different patterns of bingeing. You may need to monitor yourself using your diary for one to two weeks to get to know your own pattern.

- Once you know your pattern a bit better, try to "play around" with it a little to increase your sense of control. Try to limit your binges to just one place. Alternatively, try to restrict your bingeing to just part of the day.
- Write down a list of situations that trigger your binges and use the problem-solving approach to find ways of dealing with each one.
- Try to anticipate danger-zones. Weekends with a lot of unstructured time are prime bingeing time for many, as are journeys to and from work and lonely evenings. Draw up a timetable of pleasurable things to do during these times, such as creating and drawing from a comfort box filled with reminders of things you enjoy, and stick to it.
- When you feel like bingeing, distract yourself by doing something that is incompatible with bingeing, like going for a walk, phoning or seeing a friend. Watching television and reading are not very helpful in this respect, as you can binge at the same time. Many TV adverts are designed to promote dissatisfaction with ourselves as we are encouraged to consume more.
- Don't do your food shopping when you are feeling hungry.
- Don't ask your parents/partner/flat-mate to lock the kitchen door. This is bound to make you want the food inside more, and you will almost certainly find a way in.
- Don't blame yourself if you have had a binge. Look carefully at your behaviour chain, and spot the opportunities for new if . . . then strategies. Work through in your mind what would have happened if you had chosen a different behaviour – like making a phone call, or going for a walk, instead of opening the refrigerator. You will have learnt something for next time (go to Chapter 8, which discusses slips).
- Many people feel frightened if they haven't binged for a while. They are fearful any binge will send them back to "square one". To reassure yourself that this is not so, a useful strategy is to plan a binge, and return straightaway to your regular three meals and three small snacks a day eating pattern. A small setback can't undo the good work you have done for weeks.
- Try to avoid people, places and things that are associated with bingeing for you.

- Get in touch with someone you know who has had bulimia and has been able to control it. Find out what worked for them. See the list of support groups at the end of this book.

Coping with cravings and urges

- Monitor your urges to eat, and rate their severity (on a 1–10 scale) and duration in your diary and whether you managed to resist bingeing.
- Make a note of what effect your expected eating would have on your thoughts, feelings and physical state, as discussed in the example of Cherry:

Cherry

Cherry noticed that her urges to binge occurred when she was lonely. She had not gone out with the rest of the family but had stayed at home to study for her exams. She wrote in her diary that she expected that a binge would get rid of her feelings of loneliness and resentment about having to work. Once she had written these thoughts down, she realized that she would actually feel even more lonely and angry if she did have a binge.

When you review your diary by yourself or with your recovery guide, try to draw up a list of alternative activities that would produce the effect that you sought when you binged. In Cherry's case, while she obviously needed to study for her exams, she realized that taking regular breaks would help her feel less resentful. She also opened up to her mum about feeling lonely during her exam preparations and the mum responded very supportively.

Some of your urges to eat will be started by the normal drives of appetite in response to hunger. Others are started by environmental factors. Urges are an entirely normal reaction, and you need to develop several different strategies to deal with them.

- **Detachment**: Do not identify with the urge. Instead of thinking, "I'm dying to binge", change your thoughts to "I'm experiencing an urge to overeat – it will get strong but then it will go". Allow yourself to experience the urge, "I'll ride the wave and let it be". You don't have to give in to it. You may believe that if you don't give in to the urge, you will go mad or some other catastrophe will occur – it won't. If you do not give in to the urge, it will eventually subside and go away.
- **Imagery**: Imagine that the urge to eat is like a wave. Let yourself surf along the top of the urge without losing your balance. Don't

let the force of the wave suck you under. Imagine the urge as an alien monster. As soon as you recognise its presence, dispose of it quickly by chopping off its head.

- **Logic:** Whenever you start to think of the positive short-term benefits of binge eating, counteract these thoughts by thinking about the long-term negative consequences.
- **Distraction:** Make a list of alternative enjoyable and rewarding things you can do to take your mind off the urge.

If your trigger is anger or frustration, other ways of coping may be more helpful. An assertive response may be needed (see Chapter 11).

Lapses

Lapses will occur – they are a definite and important part of recovery. Simply regard them as challenges or learning experiences. The most important thing is to take them in your stride, and continue on the road to recovery – you took a wrong turn, easy to do, and now you are back on track.

What to do if you relapse

- **Stop and think:** Try to intervene as soon as possible, and extract yourself from the situation.
- **Keep calm:** Observe yourself with detachment. Your first reaction will be to feel guilty and blame yourself – *"How did I let this happen?"* *"I've let myself down, again"* – let these feelings ebb away. Remember, this is a normal part of recovery.
- **Renew your commitment:** Get out your balance sheet and letters, and study them again. Remind yourself of how far you have come. Remake your decision. You can be in control.
- **Review the situation that led to the lapse:** Were there early warning signals? Did you make an attempt to cope? What have you learnt for next time?
- **Take charge:** Put into play one of your coping techniques – and leave the house.
- **Get help:** Now is the time that your recovery guide can be of greatest value. Get in touch immediately. Action beats anxiety. Be brave, reach out, and resume your journey. You can do it.

Note

1   Research has shown that if you only practice a new helpful behaviour (e.g. to eat three regular healthy meals and a couple of snacks) in one particular setting (say while you are at University and supported by good friends), when you go into a different setting or environment (e.g. being at home with your parents where there are larders full of food), you are much more vulnerable to your old behaviours (bingeing) reemerging. So it is worth anticipating and planning for this.

5 Having your cake and eating it, too

You may resort to methods other than restricting food intake in an attempt to control your weight. The usual methods are making yourself vomit or taking laxatives or diuretics. Often these methods of "weight-control" start when you feel that dieting alone is not enough to counteract the binge effect. Part of you may feel, "*I can have my cake and eat it*" – however, this is far from the truth. Part of you is probably feeling deeply ashamed and worried about purging. You are right to be worried.

Facing the facts

Let's go through the facts first. How good are these methods at controlling weight? Although vomiting may get rid of 30% to 50% of calories eaten, depending on how soon this occurs after eating and on how long you have used vomiting as a regular practice, it never leads to sustained weight loss. The more you vomit, the more your body craves food. This leads to more bingeing, which makes you want to vomit more. You are caught in a vicious circle.

Laxatives and diuretics do not eliminate any calories. Yes, you are right, they may reduce weight, but this is only temporary, and is due to loss of body fluid. Your body protects against loss of water by producing hormones called anti-diuretic hormone, aldosterone, and renin, which are released generously in response to fluid loss. These hormones lead to water retention, which make you feel bloated and heavy. You may notice swelling around your eyes in the morning, in your belly, and, at the end of the day, in your ankles. These unpleasant effects make you want to increase the dose of the laxatives or diuretics you are taking. You are trapped in another vicious circle.

Taking laxatives regularly over a period of time makes your guts lazy and gives you constipation. Gradually, you have to increase the amount of laxatives you are taking. The more you take, the more constipated you become. The vicious circles become more vicious.

Why you are right to worry

Vomiting, laxatives and diuretics cause a number of health problems. You need to know about these:

• Vomiting, laxatives and diuretics lead to a loss of blood salts and water. This commonly produces CHRONIC TIREDNESS, WEAKNESS, INABILITY TO CONCENTRATE, DIZZINESS, HEADACHES and PALPITATIONS. That's not all. They also may cause EPILEPTIC FITS, IRREGULAR HEARTBEAT and KIDNEY DAMAGE.
• Stomach acid brought up by vomiting dissolves the enamel of your teeth. This makes teeth sensitive and vulnerable to cavities.
• Salivary glands around your mouth may swell because they are working overtime to produce more saliva when you vomit. Although not dangerous, this can be painful and can make your face look fat and bloated. You may look as if you have mumps. This may make you think you ought to lose more weight and may make you vomit more. Yet another vicious circle.
• Vomiting may damage your gullet. Stomach pain and vomiting blood are common. Regurgitation of food may become habitual.

- Chronic laxative use may destroy the small nerves in your gut, which may lead to gut paralysis. This is a potentially life-threatening complication, requiring surgical treatment. Your back passage may start to come down when you strain on the toilet.
- Circle which of these health problems apply to you:

Chronic tiredness	Vomiting blood
Hair loss	Dental problems
Weakness	Fits
Inability to concentrate	Irregular heartbeat
Dizziness	Constipation
Headaches	Bleeding from your bottom
Palpitations	Something coming down, down below
Stomach pain	Kidney stones
Bloating	Kidney infection
Kidney failure	Ankle swelling
Irregular periods	

Most of these problems are reversible and will improve quickly when you stop vomiting and using laxatives and diuretics. If none of these medical problems apply to you at the moment, you may feel relieved and somewhat reassured. Remember, however, that some complications take time to develop.

What type of weight controller are you?

People vary enormously in their attitudes to vomiting, laxatives and diuretics.

Type A: The vomiting behaviour is seen as a kind of physical necessity. They do not consider that they are responsible or that they have a choice. Take Carla, a 25-year-old actress, whose eating disorder started when she was 15: *"When I've binged, I feel terribly full. I feel physically sick. I'm in agony. I don't actually make myself sick. I just bend over and the food comes out. It just happens."*

Type B: The vomiting/laxatives/diuretics are a kind of habit, a part of the daily routine.

Natasha: *"Vomiting is just like brushing my teeth. I don't feel much when I do it. It makes me feel clean. I couldn't do without it."*

Lily: *"I always take five laxative tablets after every meal. I have got so used to it. I hardly think about it."*

Type C: View the purging behaviors as painful and humiliating.

Susan: *"I hate sticking my head down the loo every day. I am so ashamed of myself. How did I get into this? How could I sink so low? Afterwards,*

> *I feel totally devastated and tell myself it will never happen again. But it does and all the agony starts again."*

Sheila: *"Yesterday, I had a five-hour binge. I panicked totally and swallowed 80 laxative tablets. I spent the whole night on the loo. I was in such a lot of pain. I felt disgusted with myself and yet couldn't help feeling I somehow deserved it."*

Circle which of these types describes your own response most accurately:

Type A   Type B   Type C   Other (describe):

If type A or B describes what you feel about your vomiting, laxative or diuretic abuse, ask yourself whether you have always had this attitude. You have allowed yourself to become cut-off or detached from the pain of it. You do need to try to get in touch with these feelings again. The more cut-off you are from the negative aspects (pain, danger, shame) of your vomiting or laxative/diuretic abuse, the more difficult it will be for you to stop.

How to stop vomiting

Follow Plan A if you:

- only make yourself sick two to three times per week; or
- often induce vomiting several hours after bingeing; or
- sometimes don't vomit at all after bingeing.

Follow Plan B if you:

- vomit most days; or
- vomit after snacks, meals and binges.

Plan A: You have quite a lot of control over your vomiting, although you may not think so. The following plan is designed to give you more control.

- Look back over the past two to three weeks. What has been the maximum number of times you have been sick per week?
- Over the next week, try to be sick once less often than this maximum number.
- If you manage to do this easily, reduce the number of times of vomiting you "allow" yourself by one further episode during the second week.
- If this is difficult, repeat the same step until it becomes easier.
- Continue like this, reducing the incidents of vomiting, every week or every other week, until you stop altogether.

A tip before you start: Always write your goal for the coming week into your diary at the start of the week and try to stick to it. Try to stick to your goal exactly, but remember to make it realistic. And don't aim to change too quickly.

- If you have an extra binge, try, if at all possible, not to purge. If this is too difficult, at least try to delay the vomiting. This will make you very anxious, so use the coping techniques described under Plan B.
- If you vomit more often than you have planned for the week, return to the previous week's goal. (Remember, recovery often involves taking two steps forward and one step back.) Maybe you have been a little too ambitious, so forgive yourself and resume your recovery journey.

Plan B: You have become very used to making yourself sick as a way of dealing with or suppressing anxieties about gaining weight and perhaps other anxieties, too. To un-learn this will be difficult. At present, you probably only know two modes of existing – either being painfully full or being completely empty. Most people without an eating disorder know many states in-between, which range from being slightly hungry to being pleasantly full after a meal. You need to experience the "in-between states" again. This is best achieved by a stepwise delay of vomiting.

- Think back over the past week or two. On average, what is your time gap between eating and being sick?
- Over the coming week, try to delay being sick regularly for this length of time.
- The week after, increase the time gap a little, and so on. Move to a new, longer time-interval when you reliably achieve this week's goal.
- If you always vomit straight after eating, you may want to start with delaying vomiting for a very short time only, say 3 to 5 minutes each time. Aiming for a modest target and achieving this is better than rushing and being too ambitious – slow and steady works best on the recovery journey.

How to cope with your anxiety

Delaying a vomit will make you very anxious. You will probably feel overly full and bloated, and fears about gaining weight will rocket.

- The best technique for coping with the anxiety that arises from delaying vomiting is by treating the situation as an experiment from which new learning can arise. Write down what you expect will happen when you delay vomiting. How will it make you feel? How strong will the feeling(s) be? Rate them on a 0–10 scale. What thoughts will you have and how strongly do you believe them? Then, after you have delayed your vomiting rate, note how it made you actually feel. Was it as bad as you expected? Worse? Better? Different? Did you discover anything else about yourself?[1]

• Some people find that using social support helps them cope: for example, calling or texting your recovery guide or a friend, being with other people, or doing other activities that are engaging, such as going for a walk, or using the techniques of detachment and imagery described in Chapter 4. Stomping on an empty cardboard box, or jumping on plastic bubble wrap, bouncing a ball on the footpath – activities like these can be good fun and help to release tension. (Watching television, surfing the web, or reading are usually less successful – especially when the bathroom is close by.)

Margaret

Margaret, a 35-year-old housewife and mother of two children, enjoys needlework, and decides to use sewing as a distraction technique. Every time she feels like being sick, she tells herself that first she must knit an extra square for a patchwork blanket. "*Knitting helped me to keep my anxieties down. At the same time, to see the patchwork blanket grow makes me feel that I am channelling my anxieties into something useful.*"[2]

Judith

Judith, on the other hand, finds a spiritual solution helpful. "*Normally, I say the rosary when I want to be sick, but if the anxieties get very strong, I go to my local church and pray.*"

• Find diversions and coping strategies that work best for you. Use all your creativity and problem-solving skills for this.
• Some people write motivating, encouraging or reassuring statements on a card to carry around with them to remind them of why they embarked on the journey to recovery in the first place or to help them not to panic. Some people compose a comic song or jingle in which they make a joke of themselves. Whatever works, use it.

Elizabeth

Elizabeth is a gifted singer. On hearing that vomiting might make her hoarse, she wrote on a card, "*I want to be a singer. I don't want to damage my voice. I don't have to rely on vomiting.*" Every time she wants to be sick, she pulls out her card and reads the statements out loud to herself. "*To read the statements on the card aloud gives me more strength to resist the urge to be sick."*

Susan

Susan, who often swallowed up to 100 laxative tablets in one go, wrote a card to herself, saying, *"If I carry on like this, I will damage my health severely. I must stop."* She got this card out a few times when she felt the urge to take laxatives, but soon gave up, as thinking about the health consequences of her laxative abuse added to her sense of panic.

In writing a card, you can see from the example of Susan that writing down something that is specific to you (not a general statement) and is also positive is more effective than focusing on the negative.

Golden rules

- Try one thing at a time, for a week at a time.
- If what you have tried doesn't work, consider making things easier and try again.
- If what you have tried doesn't work, what are the "if . . . then" strategies you can rehearse and put in place?
- Especially if you follow Plan B, find ways to reward yourself when you achieve your weekly target. Otherwise, with each weekly step being small, you may have difficulty remembering that you are doing well. Compile a list of rewards and look forward to choosing one to mark your progress. Here are some suggestions to get you started:

  book
  bunch of flowers
  indoor plant
  jewellery
  train ride to the country

- Until you manage to give up vomiting completely, try to abide by this one golden tip: DO NOT BRUSH YOUR TEETH IMMEDIATELY AFTER VOMITING, as it rubs in the acid and makes things worse. Simply rinsing your mouth with either water or a bicarbonate or fluoride solution is better than brushing.

How to stop abusing laxatives, diuretics, medications

Especially if you have been taking laxatives or diuretics on a daily basis in fairly large amounts, a sudden cessation may lead to "rebound" fluid retention, which can cause gross swelling. Reducing your laxative/diuretic intake gradually may be easier for you. You can achieve this either by cutting down the number of laxatives you take each day or by slowly increasing the number of laxative/diuretic-free days per week.

Coping with constipation

Giving up laxatives will invariably make you constipated for a while. This is bound to make you feel uncomfortable and bloated. Try to be patient and remember that many women do not have a regular daily bowel movement.

Some tips to help:

- Include fruit and vegetables in your diet – this will help.
- A hot drink before eating in the morning stimulates the bowels.
- Do not eat too much bran, as this will result in stomach distention and flatulence.
- Replace laxatives on a one-to-one basis with prunes or other dried fruit.

Coping with swelling (oedema)

Despite gradually reducing your intake of laxatives/diuretics, for a while, you may remain prone to developing oedema. To prevent this:

- Consider sleeping propped up to avoid oedema collecting around your face.
- Try to sit with your legs elevated – like on a cushion or sofa – as often as you can to help the oedema drain from your ankles.

Notes and reference

1 Research has shown that what really helps new learning is if there is what is called an "expectancy violation", i.e. somehow the situation turned out differently to what you expected, such as more manageable (Craske, M.G., Treanor, M., Conway, C.C., Zbozinek, T., Vervliet, B. Maximizing exposure therapy: an inhibitory learning approach. *Behaviour Research and Therapy*, 2014 Jul;58:10–23.).

2 Interestingly, there has even been a research study that has shown that knitting distracts people with eating disorders from urges to binge. The effect is probably nothing to do with knitting per se, but with the fact that it is an activity that requires sufficient focus and degree of mental effort to engage the person, but not so fiendishly complicated that it becomes stressful. Of course, as Margaret describes, there is also the added benefit of making something useful or pretty and getting a sense of satisfaction and achievement from that.

6   Learning to feel good about your body

Many people with bulimia dislike their body intensely. They treat it as an enemy that they want to control and conquer. Do you constantly watch, criticize and struggle against your body? Many sufferers of bulimia cannot face looking at themselves naked; they cannot bear to touch their body, or for anyone else to get physically close to them or touch them. Others go to the opposite extreme and excessively check their body (visually using a variety of measuring devices and rules).

Ruth (28, pretty and petite)

When I look at myself in the mirror, I see a grotesque monster. I see the wrinkles appearing on my face, my neck is like that of an old turtle, my breasts are sagging, my stomach is huge, and my legs are flabby. My boyfriend says I have nothing to be ashamed of and other men compliment me about my appearance, but that doesn't help me feel any better about myself. When I have a bath, I lock the door so that nobody can come in and see me. I undress and wash quickly; I can't stand being naked. It is too painful. I can't bear my boyfriend near me, let alone have him touch me. We haven't made love in months. I liked to wear pretty clothes, but now I dress in big baggy jumpers to hide myself. I was a keen Morris dancer, but lately I can't face dancing anymore. I can't bear the thought of all that loose flab wobbling around.

Perhaps you don't react as strongly as this. A specific trigger may make you feel bad about your body, such as a slight weight gain, premenstrual swelling or an unwitting remark about your appearance.

Felicity

I went to work wearing a new pullover. A colleague, whom I really like, said: "That's a really nice pullover". I immediately translated that to mean "nice pullover on the wrong woman" and that he must have noticed my flat chest. For the next three days, I couldn't get rid of that thought. I avoided talking to him.

Barbara

People often shout nasty things after me as I walk along the road. I do absolutely nothing to provoke it. Most recently, I walked past a building site. As I could see some men working there, I crossed the road. They whistled and tried to get my attention. I looked straight ahead, as if I hadn't heard anything. Then one of them shouted, "She's got a fat bum". They all laughed. Whenever something like that happens, all of my insecurities about my physical appearance rise to the surface and I feel totally unattractive. If strangers bother to make comments like that about me, there must be truth in what they say, mustn't there?

The situation described by Barbara would be unpleasant for anybody. However, the reason it got to her as much as it did was linked to the fact that, as a child, she was severely bullied about her appearance by other girls at school, making her feel very insecure about herself and believing that she looked "weird". Therefore, rather than get angry with the sexist and abusive attitude shown by builders, she interpreted the men's comments as further confirmation of her own worthlessness.

Even when you encounter stresses, tensions or unpleasant events that have nothing to do with your appearance – say, your boss finds fault with your work or you have a burst pipe in your flat – you may still respond by feeling bad about your body. For many eating disorder sufferers, the way they feel about their body is the most sensitive barometer of how they feel about themselves and their life in general at a given point in time.

How body image problems are caused and maintained

Problems with body image – by this, we mean problems with your weight, shape or appearance – are a key factor in causing bulimia and in keeping it going. Therefore, it is worth trying to understand where these body problems come from and how they may "take hold" in your mind.

The role of the media and social media

A lot of research has focused on the role of the media (TV, magazines) and fashion industry in creating and maintaining body dissatisfaction in people in the Western world. From an early age, we are bombarded with pictures (usually heavily retouched and "Photoshopped") of people who are impossibly thin and glamorous, and so we learn to internalise such impossible-to-achieve thin bodies as something to aspire to. The number of radical make-over programmes, including cosmetic surgery, is also growing, creating the illusion that cosmetic surgery is an easy and straightforward way to "fix problems", and further reinforcing the idea that we all need to conform to an accepted beauty ideal.

Unsurprisingly, in this climate, most women, but increasingly also men, feel quite negative about their body at times, but especially so after looking at fashion magazines, TV advertising or other body "porn". Concerns about this have led some countries to issue government guidance (e.g. Australia, UK) or even laws (Israel) against the extremes of this (e.g. forbidding use of super skinny models) and try to educate young people to make them more media aware.[1]

Of course, social media also focus on images: for example, 20% of Facebook time is spent browsing pictures, and "likes" provide a concrete and public estimation of "value".

Online presentation is often highly managed. Up to 50% of people retouch selfies before posting them online: removing blemishes, altering skin tone or making themselves look thinner.[2] And this invites unhelpful social comparison where you just end up feeling bad about yourself.

Fat talking

Does the following sound familiar to you? A colleague of yours who is nice looking and very slim talks about looking "so fat" in her jeans and having to be really careful about not putting on more weight. You may have come across something similar at school when, after an important exam, the star pupil in your class told everyone at great length that she was worried about having failed.

This is straightforward "humble-bragging" and is a form of interaction that females tend to engage in more than men. It usually has the effect of making the listener feel utterly inadequate. At the same time, it is hard to express that to the person, as they have been so "humble".

There are other variants of fat talking, e.g. a friend telling you that she looks absolute "rubbish" in her swimming costume, whereas she assures you that you look great. Or two acquaintances talk about a third person who they have just seen in terms of "she shouldn't be wearing that at her weight or age". Fat talk may, on the face of it, seem like fairly innocent small talk, but it is actually quite corrosive and makes people feel bad about their body, and if you have an eating disorder, you may be particularly sensitive to its noxious effects.

The perils of selective attention and comparison against others

Research has shown that if people with an eating disorder look at pictures of their own body and those of other people's bodies and are asked to identify the most beautiful and the most ugly body part, and you then assess (e.g. with eye-tracking technology) how long for and how often people look at the ugly or beautiful body parts, a curious pattern emerges. People with an eating disorder will look longer and more often at the body part identified as ugly in the pictures of their own body. They do the reverse when it comes to bodies of other people. In contrast, people without an eating disorder will linger much more on the body parts they like about themselves.

You can see where this is leading – people with an eating disorder pay selective attention to the aspects of their physical appearance that they dislike and judge themselves far more harshly than others. This makes them feel bad and keeps their eating disorder going. Research also has shown that this negative assessment of one's own body leads people to expect that others will judge them negatively, too.[3] Our patients often tell us how this unfair selective attention affects them in their lives.

Also, mirrors distort our body image. If you look at yourself in a full-length mirror, your image is a much shorter version of you.

Rosie

> *Whenever I go to a social gathering or party, all I do is compare myself against all the other women in the room. Am I fatter than them? Am I less attractive? Invariably, the answer I give is "yes" and then I clam up and find it hard to talk, especially to anyone I do not know.*

Body checking, reassurance seeking and avoidance

Some people with bulimia spend ages looking in the mirror at those parts of their body they don't like and check it and check it again from different angles. Or they spend time pinching or measuring the circumference of certain body parts, such as their waist or tummy. This can become obsessive and unhelpful. This sometimes goes with repeated reassurance seeking from others (along the lines of "do I look fat in this garment?"). Yet others completely avoid looking at their body to the point where they take down mirrors or never look at themselves naked. The problem with body checking, reassurance seeking and avoidance is that while they may reduce anxiety and unhappiness about your body in the short term, in the longer term, they make you more unhappy and stuck and keep the bulimia going.

Challenging unhelpful beauty ideals and fat talk

- Go to your local art/archaeological/anthropological museum or to a library. Look at pictures or statues of women. See how their shapes have changed over the centuries and how they differ across cultures. Get some postcards or printouts of ancient Greek or Roman statues or of African tribal women. Pin them up above your bed. What do they make you feel?
- Get some evidence and make notes. Go into a cafe and watch passers-by. Maybe you could look at every seventh person who passes. What proportion are bigger or smaller than fashion images you see? Find someone who isn't slim like a fashion model and who you still think looks good. What factors do you consider in deciding if someone looks good? Their style of dress? Their posture? Their facial expression? Their way of interacting with others? Anything else?
- Now think about people you know. Again, try to think of someone who is not skinny but who you like and respect. What is it that makes them likeable in your eyes?

Notice when other people do fat talking. Notice how it makes you feel. Challenge it when you are with friends. Change the topic when you are with people you know less well. Instead, pay people real compliments. Real compliments are genuine, specific, acknowledge the other person's effort, describe the effect they have on you, use emotional language and do wait for the perfect moment.

Getting to know your body

- Close your eyes and touch and stroke your body, starting with your face, moving downwards, making sure you get a good feel of all the different parts. What do you feel? Is your skin rough or smooth, warm or cold, do you feel your heart beating, your ribcage move when you breathe, and your tummy rumble? Does touching yourself feel pleasurable or unpleasant or perhaps frightening?

- Stand against a wall. Press your shoulders and head back firmly against it. What do you feel?
- Walk around as if you are proud of your body, with your head upright. Make sure not to overstretch head or neck, as this will lead to neck ache and tension. (Walk as if you are suspended from a string.)
- Put on your favourite slow piece of music and dance gently and quietly; now switch to your favourite fast record or tape and dance as vigorously as you can, and then relax.
- Start with one inch of your body towards which you can be tender. Allow yourself to pamper this part, that is, rub in some cream or massage it. Gradually increase the area that you can treat in this way.

Looking after your body

If you don't like your body, you are likely to neglect it, be out of tune with its rhythms, and ignore its signals. Here are some suggestions to help nurture it:

- Make sure you get enough sleep at night. Allow yourself some breaks during the day. Don't drive yourself at top speed constantly.
- Draw up a list of things that you can do with, or for, your body/appearance that make you feel good. How about walking, washing windows, sunbathing, swimming, digging the garden, dancing, having a haircut, having a massage, or soaking in aromatic oils? (If your list contains mainly vigorous sports, think about whether you actually enjoy these things or whether they make you feel good mostly because they burn calories.)
- Relaxation is another excellent way to recharge body and mind. The aim is to experience a state that lies between normal, day-to-day consciousness and sleep. If you liken your mind to a car, you want to achieve the state in which it is idling, in neutral, out of gear. There are several techniques for doing this, and some will suit you better than others, so try them all. Do not expect them to be easy or to work instantly. Like any skill, such as cycling or swimming, you need to practice regularly to master it.

Other helpful strategies

Dealing with body checking, avoidance and reassurance seeking

Notice and record how often you do these behaviours and how much time you spend on them. Make a plan to reduce this, step by step. If you seek reassurance from a loved one a lot, discuss with them that it is not helpful for them to try to reassure you, as the effect quickly wears off. Instead, ask them whether they can reply as follows: "*Remember you have asked me not to reassure you. Would you like a hug instead?*" (Make up a version of this that is acceptable to you.)

Learn to accept and be compassionate to less-liked, neglected body parts

Think about your tummy that sticks out or has stretch marks, or your thighs that are big, or your bum that you think is too "saggy". Write a letter to this body part and tell it what you think about it. Then write a letter back from this body part. Get it to speak up for itself. What is it doing for you? How is it helping other parts of your body to work? What function does it have? How has it supported you?

Coming to terms with the origins of your body image problems

Are they related to earlier experiences, e.g. your big brothers always teasing you about your weight or shape, or someone having bullied you at school? First, write a letter to that person and let them know how you feel about what they have said and done. If you think that the person who teased/bullied you might now have insight into their behaviour, write a letter back as if from them, apologising for what they have done. Finally, write a compassionate letter to your younger self (i.e. at the age when the teasing or bullying happened). What protective or comforting things could you say to yourself? Review all letters. How does that make you feel?

Living with your body

Living with/inside a body you don't like is difficult. Many of the people we see avoid getting on with their lives: they don't go out, they shelve or avoid relationships, and . . . and . . . and . . . . They dream the same dream. "If only I . . . were slimmer, less pear-shaped, had thinner thighs, not such a big tummy . . . my life would be completely different." Some people waste years like this, existing but not really living.

Tragically, in the early phase of an eating disorder, some people achieve their ideal appearance for a short while through following a punishingly hard diet, and often this is remembered years later as the one good period, the pinnacle in their life that they want to return to at all cost. Only rarely do people allow themselves to remember the personal cost.

Jane

> *If I am honest, my life wasn't all rosy when I weighed 98 lbs. I thought about food day and night. I dreamt about it and sometimes had nightmares about being force-fed. I felt guilty about absolutely anything I ate, I couldn't eat an apple without regretting it. I argued a lot with my boyfriend. I was very irritable and lost my interest in music. Although many people commented on how pretty I looked, my closest friends began to think I had undergone a personality change. I kept getting distracted, I couldn't concentrate, and I couldn't look at them when they talked to me. They didn't like this "me" at all.*

When you have an eating disorder, you tend to overestimate the size of your body, and the more out of control your eating is, the worse this gets. Working on your eating behaviour, therefore, will have a positive effect on your attitudes to your body. However, attitudes are far harder to change than behaviour, and they change far more slowly. So, even when you manage to get into a pattern of eating normally fairly quickly, your negative body image is likely to persist for a while longer. Be patient. You can't change everything overnight.

What you can do, however, is work on those things you avoid due to feeling bad about your body. What is the point of wasting more time? Let's get on with your recovery journey.

Susan

Susan made a list of all the things that she avoided. She wrote them down in hierarchical order, starting with the situations she feared most, progressing to the ones she feared least but still avoided. Here is her list:

- swimming/going to the beach in a bikini (impossible)
- dancing a slow dance with a man (very difficult to get physically close to someone)
- going to a party (difficult to meet new people and to know what to talk about)
- dining in a restaurant with friends (worried what they will think about me if they see me eat)
- wearing tight skirts (worried about my stomach and lack of waist)
- wearing short sleeved T-shirts (my arms are flabby)
- wearing brightly-coloured clothes (fear this will draw attention to me)

Make a similar list for yourself. Tackle an easy situation over the next week and a slightly more difficult one the week after. Include this challenge list in your weekly goals.

If you go ahead with this, don't expect to find it easy or to enjoy yourself at all initially. Expect to have a difficult, anxious and very self-conscious time. It will take quite a bit of time before you can hope to feel more at ease with yourself. Getting better is about taking some risks. What do you have to lose?

Notes and references

1 http://www.ncb.org.uk/media/861233/appg_body_image_final.pdf
2 http://renfrewcenter.com (2013)
3 Alleva, J., et al. *Appetite*, 2013 Sep;68:98–104.

7 Being fatter may be better

If, in addition to bulimia, you have a problem with your weight, and exceed the top end of the weight band for your height (see Table 3.1, Chapter 3), this chapter is especially for you.

In our society, to be round in shape and happy in spirit at the same time is difficult. Long gone are the days of Rubens and fulsome-figured actresses like Marilyn Monroe and Jane Russell. If your weight puts you in the heavy half of the population, you are likely to feel under constant pressure to go on a diet and lose weight. Messages via social media, magazines, television, acquaintances and even friends may make you feel morally inferior unless you at least are seen to be trying to conform to society's idealised norms.

Josie

> *I was a big child, and a big teenager. I weigh 252 lbs now. For years, I have been subjected to comments, abuse and humiliation. Because I am over-weight, people think they have the right to criticize me. Like, the other day, my ear was aching and I saw a new GP. He briefly dealt with my ear, proceeded to lecture at length on the health risks of being overweight, and referred me to a dietician.*

Josie also notes:

> *As long as I am seen trying to lose weight, others are pleased, and offer encouragement. But if I'm seen eating an ice-cream or piece of cake in pub-lic, people say: "Oh, I thought you were on a diet? Aren't you a bit naughty? Think of how nice you could look if you lost a bit of weight." Even if they say nothing, the disapproval is evident in their faces. I can see they think: "She's letting herself go".*

Sadly, obesity is one of the most stigmatized physical attributes in Western society, discriminated against in a wide range of settings. In 1992 in the United States, women's groups started to rebel against the diet dictators and began to smash weighing scales with the slogan, "*Scales are for fish, not women*". Some organisations are trying to counteract the stigma of obesity by advocating greater acceptance of diversity in body shapes and sizes (Health at Every Size[1]; National Association for the Advancement of Fat Acceptance[2]).

Health risks in being overweight

We are pummelled with the powerful message that when we are heavy, we are damaging our health. Many diets are started on medical recommendation. Public health campaigns have emphasised that obesity is linked to heart disease, high blood pressure, diabetes, joint problems and certain sorts of cancer. However, scientists now think that the seriousness of these risks has been exaggerated, cer-tainly for people who are only mildly or moderately overweight. Being plump may actually offer some protection against some forms of disease. Newer research shows that it is not high weight, as such, but rather your weight yo-yoing up and down – as is common for many people who regularly diet – that may lead to heart disease and death. People who are heavy and fit probably don't have more health risks than those who are thinner.

Nothing beautiful about dieting

You may say: "*That's all very well, but I can't wait until society is more accepting of my kind of figure. I want to feel accepted; I want to lose weight. Now.*" Remem-ber the message from Chapter 3: diets don't work. Besides being ineffective, dieting will increase the likelihood of you starting to binge eat. Your weight will start to bounce up and down. This instability will lead to harmful metabolic patterns, with swings of insulin, fat and sugar, and ultimately to your weight creeping up more and more. Remember: a diet begun with the aim of improving health and beauty will have the opposite effect. You will feel worse instead of better.

Samantha

Samantha, a 23-year-old beautician, gained more than 30 kg during a three year-period, when she began a stringent diet and progressed into the yo-yo cycle of binge eating. Her weight gradually went up, and up (see Figure 7.1).

The painful but simple truth is that you have to stop dieting to get over binges and to allow your weight to settle to a level that is right for you. To acknowledge and accept this is extremely difficult. Monitoring your eating pattern in a diary, as we have introduced earlier, is an essential first step. Structuring your daily intake with three regular meals and three snacks is essential.

Alison

Alison, 24, could not control her eating. She would diet for a day or two and spend the rest of the week bingeing. Then a therapist told her that, to stop bingeing, she would need to eat three meals a day plus three snacks daily, and that she could eat anything she wanted for those meals and snacks.
Alison said:

I was amazed at this solution. I realised that I had not been eating what I wanted for nearly all my adult life. I had swung from one diet to another, and here I was being told to eat regularly, and to eat anything I wanted,

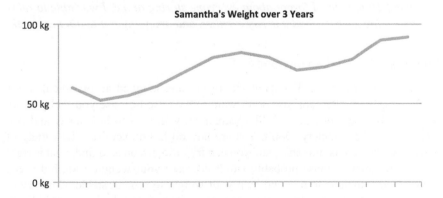

Figure 7.1 Samantha's weight chart.

including potatoes, puddings and sweets. I was totally surprised when, after a week of doing this, I had lost 7 lbs. I did not go on losing weight, but managed to maintain it, which was the first time I had done that for many years. After several months, when I was comfortable with eating regularly, my therapist suggested that it might be safe for me to cut down slightly. The way I did this was to make sure that I did not eat much more than 1700 calories a day. All this meant was that I did not eat huge great portions of anything, but could continue eating all my favourite foods.

Avoiding the lonely trap

Because of the stigma of being fat, secondary problems can arise with your daily lifestyle, career, social and family life and contribute to the downward spiral. You may have put your life completely on "hold", not wanting or feeling worthy of any form of pleasure or enjoyment while you are fat. Subjecting yourself to loneliness and misery because of what you think others will say is a sure recipe for disaster and will exacerbate your alienation. The solution is to start setting goals and structuring each day so that you are in the driver's seat of your life.

Samantha

Samantha, introduced earlier in this chapter, was so upset by her weight gain that she stopped working as a beautician. She felt inferior to the other women working in the salon, and could no longer fit into her uniform. She restricted her social life more and more and only left home to go shopping by car. She felt miserable and alone. With encouragement from her therapist, Samantha decided to try going out and socialising at least once a week, although the thought of this terrified her. The following week, Samantha reported back to her therapist:

I did it. I went out to the pub. I felt very nervous, and when I got there, I felt that everyone was looking at me, seeing how fat, ugly and horrible I was. But my friend was with me, and we sat at a corner table and, do you know, after about 10 minutes, I forgot about everyone staring at me. I was able to relax and enjoy myself. I had a lovely evening, and am going out again next week.

Shake, shake, shake your body

Perhaps you always hated sport at school or were laughed at, or ridiculed, for performing badly. Perhaps you don't want to exercise because you feel you are not the right shape or size and, like Samantha, you want to hide away and isolate yourself from society. Don't. You are not too fat to exercise. The variety of activities available is immense, and you can try different ones to find what is right for you. Regular exercise probably won't decrease your weight a lot, but it can increase your metabolic rate and help your weight to remain stable. Contrary to common belief, exercise does not increase appetite but slightly decreases it. Exercise also increases suppleness, strength and stamina. An ideal de-stressor, it can take your mind off your problems and, after a session of exercise, you will feel warm, comfortable and relaxed. Exercise is a great alternative to overeating or purging, which, for many people with eating disorders, are prime ways of coping with stress. It also can ease depression and help sleep.

Remember, exercise can:

1. Promote health and fitness.
2. Provide a sense of mastery, enhance a sense of well-being and reduce stress, tension or low mood.
3. Help your weight to stabilise rather than continue to go up.
4. Preserve body muscle.

Overcoming obstacles

- Perhaps, like many people with an eating disorder, you have an "all-or-nothing" approach to life, and jump in at the deep end and do something to excess, which is painful and uncomfortable, and then avoid it. A better approach is to be like the tortoise – start with something that you enjoy and build up the intensity slowly and gradually. Exercise does not need to cause pain to be good for you. If it does cause pain, you are pushing yourself too hard. If your breathing is uncomfortable, slow down.
- The need to please others and a fear of being selfish, which are other characteristics of people with eating disorders, may lead you to think that you have not got time to devote to something that is primarily for yourself. You do not need a lot of time. Just 20 minutes, two to three times per week, can be sufficient. Persevere, and you are likely to find that putting this time aside not only becomes easier but is also something you look forward to.
- Even if you have young children, you can find a way of getting more exercise. Many sport and leisure centres have childcare facilities, and you can get details from your local council leisure and recreation department or your local library.
- Try to incorporate your children into your exercise schedule, as this role modelling will set up good habits for them. Take them in a pram or stroller when you go for long walks, put them on your bicycle or play with them in the pool.
- Perhaps you can think of doing something that involves someone else. Can you persuade a friend to accompany you on a regular walk, or join a yoga club or a water aerobics class?
- Try to choose something that fits into your routine easily, so you can do it regularly. Don't take on something for which you have to travel far or that you can do only under certain weather conditions.

- If you are overweight, the self-defeating "I-don't-fit-in-or-belong" outlook on life (described in Chapter 10) can lead you to avoid exercise, due to fear of looking ridiculous or being mocked and teased by others. Although an ignorant minority will always think this way, people whose views you respect will commend your initiative and your bravery in facing a challenge and doing something positive. This is far better than avoiding the problem.
- If you have a medical condition such as a heart problem or joint problems or simply are worried about whether exercise is right for you, discuss it with your general practitioner. There are, however, very few people for whom moderate exercise is dangerous.

How to change your lifestyle to get fitter

An "all-or-nothing" or "either I am perfect or I am useless" approach to life is self-defeating in the context of exercise. You do not have to start marathon running. Slight changes in your lifestyle can achieve an increase in mobility and stamina – you can start by walking more and increasing your physical activity around your home and work environment.

The challenge is to find new ways of doing the things you usually do. Don't save things up to be efficient, do them as you think of them. You will feel better, being on the move.

Walking

Walking is excellent and readily available, with few risks of injury or strain. Use your walk time to observe, reflect and file thoughts, listen to music, learn a language or talk with a friend.

Put on a pair of reasonably comfortable shoes, and you are ready to start. For a little prior pampering, put talcum powder on your feet (and tights), and afterwards, persuade a friend to give you a foot massage or run a bath, add some aromatic oil, and soak in it for 10 minutes.

Begin walking for 15 minutes each day, increasing by five minutes each day or week. If the 15-minute walk is too difficult, go for a shorter period initially. Aim to walk for one hour each day.

Experiment to find the best combination of place, time and companionship for you.

Walking with a partner can be an excellent time for talking together without distractions that can occur in the home. Talking while you are walking with a friend provides time to unwind and to mull things over. Walking with a dog is rewarding, too, and the dog certainly will remind you "it's walk time". However, if a companion is not available, walking alone is a real joy, too. You do not need to hold someone's hand, or a dog leash, to walk regularly around the block.

Walking burns off the same number of calories as running the same distance. The distance you go is more important than how fast you go.
Think of ways to include more walking in your life:

- Get up 30 minutes early to walk.
- Walk during lunch breaks.
- Walk after work.
- Walk before bed.
- Park your car at the longest distance from the shopping centre door.
- Get on/off your bus or trainstop one stop early.
- Consider joining a walking group such as the Ramblers[3] or Walking for Health.[4]

Try to include walking in your daily pattern of life, but don't despair if you miss an occasional day. Try to plan your holidays with walking opportunities in mind.

Using stairs

Climbing stairs burns more calories per minute than vigorous activities like jogging and cycling. Incorporating the use of stairs into your lifestyle is easy because you can find stairs almost everywhere – at home, at work, in shops and on public transport. In modern buildings, you may need to do some detective work to find the stairs, but they will be there. Research has shown that regular stair climbing leads to better fitness, less body fat, trimmer waistlines and a drop in blood pressure. Spending about 10 minutes a day going up or down stairs five times a week reduces risk of death from any cause by about 15%.[5]

Avoid using the lift whenever possible, or take it to the floor below where you have to go, so that you walk up the last flight. Use every opportunity to go up and down the stairs at home or at work. Try to ensure that you have to use stairs to go to the toilet or to make a drink. Be creative in finding new ways to take more steps in the normal course of your day.

Measuring your goals

Technology has made it easier for us to measure our progress with exercise. Many gadgets are available to measure the number of steps taken during walking, the energy expended in terms of calories burnt, and record pulse and blood pressure. Many of these can be synced with your computer or phone to download your "statistics" over time. Build up your walking to 10,000 steps a day. This may sound like a lot, but most of us walk between 3,000 and 4,000 steps a day anyway and you can walk about 1,000 steps in 10 minutes, so this is less daunting than it seems.

Here is how some people with eating disorders have increased their exercise:

Samantha

Samantha was initially very pessimistic about trying to increase her exercise. She re-enrolled at an aerobics class that she had attended before she gained weight and was deeply upset to find that she could not keep pace with even the easiest exercises in the class. Her therapist explained that she needed to start exercising very gradually and, between them, they decided Samantha's initial aim should be 10 minutes' brisk walking a day:

When my therapist suggested 10 minutes' walking a day, I thought that was absolutely hopeless. I felt that I ought to be exercising really, really hard for hours and hours or not bother to do anything at all. My therapist explained that my body would take time to readjust to exercise and that it was best to build up gradually. I was sceptical, but went along with it, as I had been so upset that I could not do the aerobics. What I started doing was go out for a walk in the evening with my friend at dusk when I felt people were not likely to see me. We would walk for a little bit, and then I would say that it was time to do my 10 minutes' brisk walking, so I would increase the speed for this 10 minutes, and then we would slowly walk back to the house. Soon, this became less of a challenge, and so I began to build up the brisk walking time by five minutes each week. Just going out of the house for my regular evening walk made me feel less sensitive about people seeing me, and I started going out for walks during the daytime as well. I felt good doing something positive about my problem instead of just sitting, waiting for it to go away.

Claire

Claire, 29, found exercise difficult to do, as she worked as a telephonist and spent most of her day sitting down:

I just did not know how to fit exercise into my day. Then I had the idea of getting off the bus one stop early and walking that last bit to work. I was amazed how exhausted I felt for the first few days. Perseverance paid off though and, as walking became easier, I began getting off the bus two stops earlier, then three stops and now, a year and a half later, I am cycling to work. I feel so good when I cycle past the bus and see pale, pasty faces in the window and think, "that used to be me".

Some exercises to do at home

Many people prefer to exercise at home. Perhaps you do, too. It's private, and there's no need to get a babysitter or travel anywhere. The NHS Choices website has a wealth of resources covering aerobic exercise, strength and resistance training, and pilates and yoga, and how you can gradually build up your activity levels, all of which you can download for free.[6] You can also take an online test that helps you to figure out which type of exercise might be most enjoyable and suited for you.

Venturing out

Swimming: this exercise is good for increasing strength, stamina and suppleness.[7] Swimming is particularly good if you are heavy or have some disability, as the water supports your body and there is no strain on your joints. Many local swimming pools have special sessions for women only or women with toddlers. There are often concession rates, or you can buy a season ticket. Get in touch with your local authority leisure department.

Susan

> Susan had always been heavy, but after the birth of her child, her eating pattern became chaotic, and her weight increased. She had always been quite active but, as she became more ashamed of her body, she went out less. When encouraged to take up swimming, she was reluctant. She said she would feel ashamed to undress in public. However, she went to see what was available at her local swimming pool and leisure centre. They did not have sessions for women only, but they did have an early-morning session. Susan enrolled for this. She wore a long T-shirt over her bathing costume and found, at that early time, most people at the pool were sleepy and preoccupied and did not notice her. She was able to go three times a week before her husband left for work.

Once you become more active, you may want to diversify your exercise programme.

Cycling: good for stamina and leg strength. If you can't afford a new bike, look online for a secondhand one. Bikes are easy to store and maintain, and you can cycle safely along bike tracks, in local parks or join a club.

Jogging and running: popular, but you can develop over-use injury to your lower limbs, so try to run on soft surfaces and with good shoes. You can join clubs that cater for all levels of performance, and offer social events as well. Again, the NHS Choices website has great information on how to build up your running time safely.[8]

Golf: some local authorities have public courses that are reasonably priced.

Bowling: indoors or outdoors, this is a sociable sport, and clubs are growing with recruits of all ages.

Racket sports: some, like badminton, are good for beginners and can be played at evening classes or local clubs.

Weight training: more and more women are entering into this, but learn how to do it safely by joining a class at your local leisure centre.

Martial arts and judo: many clubs are available, but make sure that they belong to the national governing body.

Exercise classes (yoga, movement and dance): check that the class you choose starts at the right level for you. Start with a beginners' class. Getting on with the teacher is important, too – not everybody will – and it is okay if you need to change classes.

Notes and references

1 http://www.haescommunity.org/
2 http://www.naafaonline.com/dev2/the_issues/index.html
3 http://www.ramblers.org.uk/
4 http://www.walkingforhealth.org.uk/
5 Meyer, P., et al. Stairs instead of elevators at workplace: Cardioprotective effects of a pragmatic intervention. *European Journal of Cardiovascular Prevention & Rehabilitation*, 2010 Oct;17(5):569–575.
6 http://www.nhs.uk/Conditions/nhs-fitness-studio/Pages/welcome-to-nhs-fitness-studio.aspx
7 http://www.nhs.uk/Livewell/getting-started-guides/Pages/getting-started-swimming.aspx
8 http://www.nhs.uk/Livewell/c25k/Pages/get-running-with-couch-to-5k.aspx

8 Relapse

Walking in circles – or not

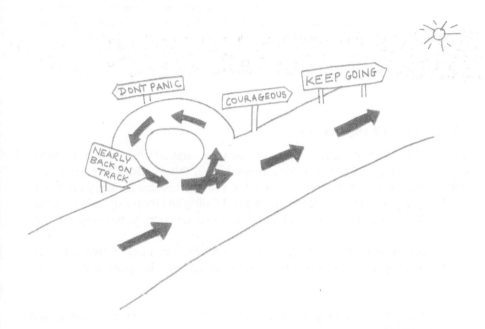

Your eating disorder may remain your Achilles' heel, your vulnerable spot, for the rest of your life. Constant vigilance will help you to avoid being tripped up when you least expect it. You need to know how to prevent slips from occurring and what to do if a slip occurs. In this chapter, we provide some strategies.

Preventing slips

Plan your own relapse

Recovery from an eating disorder involves facing numerous setbacks before the eating problem subsides. Everyone on the recovery journey confronts obstacles at some time or another. Knowing this can help you not to panic about the prospect of having a slip. Many people find, when they haven't binged and vomited for a while, that they get increasingly anxious and worried that a setback might strike at any moment and hit them harder than ever. (Do you recognise this unhelpful thought? See more on this subject in Chapter 10.) One practical way of dealing with this anxiety is to plan a relapse. No, we are not having you on: bringing on, deliberately, what you fear most is an excellent way to increase self-belief.

- Set aside some time, buy your favourite binge foods, and have a binge. Spread all the food out on the table, and eat as much as you can. Focus on your binge as fully as you can. Can you bring yourself to stuff the food down in your usual fashion? Can you bring yourself to eat as much of each food as in the past? How does it feel? Is this really the worst thing that can happen to you? At the end of this binge, do you feel you are back to square one?
- Repeat this exercise at least once a month if you feel worried that you are doing too well.

What to do if a slip occurs

After a slip, it is easy to think the worst, be your harshest critic and loathe yourself. You perhaps think that having slipped once, this confirms you are a total failure and will never recover. You may tell yourself that the recovery journey is too hard, and that the discomfort of trying and failing and trying again is too much to bear. We suggest that, instead of thinking this way, you try to be compassionate to yourself.

Self-compassion is a way of positively relating to oneself that does not involve judging yourself or comparing yourself against other people. It has three components:

- Self-kindness, i.e. thinking about yourself and your actions with warmth and understanding.
- Being aware that mistakes, suffering and unfairness are part of the human condition.
- Neither ignoring nor ruminating on disliked aspects of oneself or one's actions/life.

So what does that mean in practice if you have slipped? Don't hate or despise yourself. Remind yourself of your good intentions. You have been trying hard to make changes and recover. Think of what you can learn from the slip. Keep things in perspective. This is just a slip and you can do something about it.

Add pleasure to your day

Many women, especially women with an eating disorder, devote much time to caring for other people's needs, at work, in the family and in their social network, and have great difficulty looking after their own needs, or even recognising that they have needs and wants. An imbalance between "should", those activities that you see as chores or things you feel obliged to do, and "want", those activities

Learning from slips

Try to stand back from how you feel about your lapse, and take an honest look at how it actually came about. Don't say: *"It just happened"*. There is always a reason. Ask yourself the following questions:

- Are you keeping to the dietary ground-rules outlined in Chapter 3? Are you eating three meals and three snacks daily? Are you allowing yourself to eat enough at mealtimes? Have you omitted meals or left long gaps between them?
- Does bingeing still seem the easiest and quickest source of comfort and pleasure in your life? If so, you need to make life changes so you can develop healthy, safe ways of being contented and relieving pressure.
- Did stress, upset, unhappiness, anxiety or any other unpleasant feeling cause your lapse? If so, list other ways you can deal with these triggers.

The more carefully you think about your lapse, the more it can teach you and can help you to make different plans, either to stop feeling tempted or to cope differently if temptation arises. Don't try to ignore a slip and rely on your willpower to change.

Take active steps to change the behaviour and address the situations that act as triggers. Ask your recovery guide and others to help make these changes.

Remember, if you slip, you have the power within you to decide whether to continue to binge eat and have a complete relapse or whether to stop the episode. Right now.

engaged in for self pleasure, is often responsible for relapse. "Should" and "want" are subjective, depending on pressures and circumstances. Table 8.1 overleaf shows the diary of Isabel, a young solicitor.

You can see that most of Isabel's day is made up of "should". The only "want" she allows herself is food-related, and this is concentrated at the end of the day. Do you recognise this? Does food, when you allow yourself to have it, give you this much thrill or comfort? Often women with eating disorders find overeating difficult to give up, as this constitutes the only nurturing or pleasure in their life (and the one pleasure that is most easily accessible).

Table 8.1 Isabel's "should" and "want" diary

Activity	Should	Want
Get up	+	
Drive to work	+	
Deal with e-mails & phone calls	+	
3 appointments	+	
Running late, no time for lunch	+	
Go to bank	+	
Writing reports	+	
2 further clients	+	
Shop – buy biscuits & chocolate to eat in the car		+ +
Drive home	+	
Make self sick		+
Tidy flat	+	
Iron clothes	+	
Finish reports for work	+	
Supper		+
Binge		+

- Draw up your own "should list" and "want list" diary for a week.
- Do you find the "shoulds" take over your life? We encourage you to create a balance so that you are caring for yourself as well as others. Self-care needs to incorporate activities that nurture both your mind and body.
- What can you do to achieve more balance in your life?
- What can you do to comfort and excite yourself, besides eating?
- Make a list of your "wants" and desires. Include big and small things on your list: wild, decadent dreams like "a three-week holiday in a luxury hotel in Barbados", and some simple things like "10 minutes to myself every morning to do some relaxation". Start with the small things, and make sure you incorporate at least one 'want' or desire in every day. Start now.

9 Childhood wounds

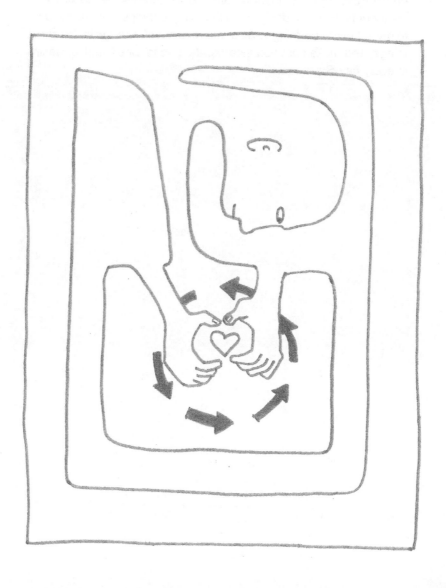

Your childhood may have lacked the safe, consistent loving and nurturing experience that every child deserves. A proportion of children who go on to develop an eating disorder have been raised in an environment where there is problematic or inadequate parenting, physical and emotional abuse, and sexual abuse. This can be the result of the parents splitting up or a parent dying, or may stem from psychological problems in a parent, like depression or alcohol abuse.

Sometimes the problems are less overt. You may have felt your parents had little time or energy for you, that they lacked interest in you, were physically or emotionally unavailable to you; perhaps they were preoccupied with their work or were depressed due to a family crisis such as marriage breakdown. Or maybe they gave you the feeling that you would be accepted only if you met their expectations of what they wanted you to be; and felt that you would be liked and loved only if you wore the clothes they wanted you to wear, followed the career path they wanted you to follow, and were good, successful or clever. Lack of approval and withheld affection can leave profound scars, with later difficulties in relationships. Early experiences like this can change the way your genetic code is read, which impacts on the stress response, making you more sensitive to any stress you experience.

Sandra

Sandra grew up in South Africa. Her parents split up when she was four. Her mother then remarried. The stepfather drank heavily. When he was drunk, he would beat Sandra and her two sisters or force them to drink whisky. There were incessant arguments between him and their mother. Sandra repeatedly witnessed her stepfather beating her mother:

We were terrified when they fought. I often feared he would kill my mother.

Most of the time, Sandra was left completely on her own, to survive as best she could. The family had servants, one of whom forced Sandra to have sexual intercourse on several occasions. He threatened to kill her if she told her parents. When Sandra was 12 years of age, her mother left the stepfather, and Sandra was sent to England to live with her natural father:

At first, I wanted to live with him. In fact, when I still lived with my mother and stepfather, I often dreamt that Dad would come and rescue me. But once I began living with him, our relationship became stressful. He was quite strict and tried to make me work as well as attend school. He was often critical of the way I dressed and of my friends; he inferred that I didn't study hard enough at school. He probably tried his best to get on with me, but I was fairly rebellious in my early teens, and I didn't trust him enough.

Such negative childhood experiences often produce low self-esteem, depression, suppressed anger, or open rebellion and difficulties in developing trusting relationships. Instead of adopting a "give-and-take" middle ground in your relationships, you may find yourself fluctuating between extreme positions where you either idealise people, putting them on a pedestal, or feel totally negative about them. This leads to loneliness or feeling let down or ignoring your own needs.

Do you recognise some of the following experiences in your childhood?

- Did you have to fend for yourself as your parents were absent or preoccupied; did you therefore have to grow up before your time? Did you need to take responsibility for yourself, and perhaps look out for and care for others in the family as well?
- Were you ruled with an iron rod, with fear of violence to yourself or to others? You may have been left feeling crushed, resentful or rebellious.
- Did you feel loved and accepted only when you met certain standards in looks, behaviour or achievement?
- Did you feel that your parents were perfect? Were you and your parents best friends? This kind of bond may make it difficult for you to reach out and explore other relationships.
- Did you feel that you were envied? Did you have better chances, at education for instance, than others? Were you considered the "capable" child in the family? Did this make you deny and spoil your opportunities?
- Did you feel that your physical and emotional needs were neglected or damaged? Were you used as a scapegoat for your parents' feelings of anger or dissatisfaction?

You may find it helpful to reflect on your early environment in a more focused way. Be mindful, however, that this type of reflective project might be associated with pain. We suggest, for this process to be healing, you probably need the perspective of a compassionate, trusted recovery guide to help you build the broader context and to embed this with mature memories and knowledge.

- Draw your family tree.
- What are your memories of your early family life? Perhaps you can jot some things down. For example, how did your family deal with:

  - relatives
  - mealtimes/celebrations
  - school/friends
  - religion/authority figures
  - money/talents/gifts
  - illness/losses

- Write your life story. Do any points mentioned here jog a memory? From your vantage point now as an adult, can you see the bigger picture and understand more the events shaping the reactions of people around you? Zoom back to yourself as a child with a child's understanding. How did you make sense of what happened then? What did you learn about emotions, yourself, others and relationships? Share your story with your recovery guide.

Sexual abuse

Sexual abuse in childhood is a form of trauma that may be particularly difficult to come to terms with because of the aura of secrecy, shame and stigma that surrounds it.

What is sexual abuse?

Child sexual abuse happens when an adult or older person touches or uses a child in a sexual way. This can include many different kinds of behaviors but the main thing is that, by being bigger, stronger or having power or authority in the child's life, the adult can trap, lure, force or bribe them into sexual activity.

How do I know if I have been sexually abused?

Sexual abuse of a child can occur when you are:

- cuddled or kissed in a way that left you feeling uncomfortable
- bathed in a way that made you feel uneasy
- made to watch sexual acts or look at other people's genitals
- shown sexual films or videos, or forced to listen to sexual talk
- made to pose for "sexual" photographs
- touched on your breasts or genitals
- made to touch an adult's or older person's genitals
- made to have oral sex
- penetrated (having the adult thrust a finger, his penis or an object inside your vagina or anus)
- raped (penetrated using force or violence).

Other less obvious things may have been done or said to you that have deeply affected you, and that you have found abusive.

Why is it wrong?

This form of early sexual activity is wrong because it hurts the victim, sometimes physically, but more often psychologically. We know that it can cause confusion, fear, anger, shame, self-blame and leave the victim with a very low opinion of themselves. Without help, the victim can sometimes experience serious problems in adult life.

Such early sexual activity is abusive and deeply wrong because every person should have a right to decide what happens to their body. Adults should normally protect that right for children and young people, so any situation where physical force is used or threatened, or where the person feels they can't say "no", can be called sexual assault. Children and young people, for many reasons, can't really say "no" to adults, nor have they the power to stop them. Young children do not even understand what is happening. The adult in this situation is always committing a crime. About 10% of women in the community and 30 to 40% of women with eating disorders have been sexually abused in their childhood or raped in later life. The spectrum of abuse ranges from one-off experiences to repeated abuse over years. Any form or incidence of sexual abuse constitutes a gross exploitation of a power relationship. Often the abuser is a member of the family or someone known to the family.

Trying to make sense of it

Victims of sexual abuse commonly feel that they are to blame for what happened, that they allowed the abuse to happen or somehow provoked, encouraged or deserved it. Physical force or psychological threats are often used to silence the victim and are designed to confuse you by making you feel that you are in the wrong, or as if you invited the advances. If you are brave enough to discuss the abuse with a trusted adult, you are often met with disbelief, told "don't be silly", and the whole thing gets hushed up in the family. Often the perpetrator goes on living within the family or continues to be welcomed as a regular visitor.

Hazel

Hazel was sexually abused when a young child for a number of years by her father's brother. She often stayed with this uncle and his wife for the summer holidays.

When my aunt was out doing the shopping, he would often ask if I wanted him to read a story. He would sit me on his lap and begin to touch me up, my genitals, my breasts. I could feel that he had an erection. I had a sense that this was wrong. I didn't ask him to stop. I didn't tell my parents at the time.

Hazel eventually mustered up the courage to tell her parents about this when she was 16. *My mother was very good about it, but my father, I think, still doesn't believe me. He accused me of lying and got very cross with me. I think he was totally shocked that something like this could happen in his family. I never visit my uncle now. My parents still go because they don't want open conflict in the family. I am afraid that because my uncle abused me, he could abuse another child, too.*

Many victims of sexual abuse feel that the abuse completely changed the way they feel about themselves as a person and that they have been left with a wound, like a hole in their soul, that will never heal. Kathy, whose father repeatedly raped her when she was in her teens, said: *"It feels like a poison growing inside me."*

- If you have been sexually abused and have received no support, talking about this at the moment may seem too difficult – or you might decide you want to do something about it right now.
- First, we encourage you to read other sufferers' experiences of abuse. You will not feel so alone, full of shame and different to everyone else. You have done nothing wrong and deserve to be treated with respect.

At the end of this book, you will find a reading list that may be of interest to you. Order the titles that interest you from your local library, or download them online.

- You may want to talk to someone anonymously about your (often long-suppressed) experience of sexual abuse. Self-help lines are available (unfortunately, they are often busy).
- We suggest you write down what happened to you, as though describing a court scene, as if this awful experience happened to someone else. Write down what the prosecuting lawyer for the victim would say. He might set his case out by addressing the following points:

  - How did the abuse start?
  - What ways did the abuser use to ensure you kept their abuse of you secret?
  - How long did the abuse continue?
  - What were the worst things about it?
  - What did the abuser do?

- Write down what you predict the defence lawyer for the perpetrator might say.
- Write down the jury's response, and finally, the judge's speech.
- Do you feel you can share your story with someone? Your recovery guide, maybe? They may be able to help complete the lawyer's case, give more of the jury's verdict, and ensure that the judge was wise. If the victim of the story were your own child, would your arguments differ?

Trying to understand and make sense of what happened to you can lead to confusing feelings that can fester for many years. Try to answer these questions:

- Do you blame yourself for the abuse? Who else is to blame?
- Do you have secret fears about yourself? Or about others?
- If you are angry, what are you angry about? Who are you feeling angry at?
- If you feel scared, what are you scared about?
- The situation gets particularly confusing if, apart from the abuse, you have some good memories and feelings about the abuser. This doesn't indicate that you are a monster. Children naturally try to see the good in things and in people. What were the good memories? Do you have good memories you want to keep?
- Similarly, many victims are left with mixed feelings about their parents. What are your good and bad feelings towards your parents?
- Rank the strength of your feelings on a scale of 1 to 10.
- Draw yourself and other members of the family. See how you draw them and note the feelings these drawings evoke in you.
- Record your feelings in your diary, and do the ABC detective work as outlined in Chapter 2.

The right to be angry

Anger is a natural response to abuse, but you may have learnt that getting angry leads to more abuse, or that you are not allowed to feel or express anger. You may have witnessed terrible violence done in anger and therefore think this emotion must be suppressed.

The abuser often stifles or deflects the victim's anger and it is turned inwards, therefore, you feel bad or you take your anger out on yourself by hurting yourself or deadening your anger with food. Is it fair to continue to add to the burden of hurt and pain carried by the child victim inside you?

What can you do with angry feelings?

Recognising your anger and how you cope with it and understanding the implications that this has for you in terms of your needs, values and life plans is a project that should be embarked upon with skills and support.

First, in order to do this, you may need to build up skills in shifting the attentional focus of your mind because when emotions are too hot, the brain switches from reflective to automatic mode. You can only learn and form mature understanding from the reflective mode. You therefore need the ability to focus on the anger and then be able to switch attention and ground yourself in a calm present.

Often anger is linked to sadness and so you need to also have the ability to switch to a pleasant, nurturing mindset. This is an important life skill that takes time, practice and patience to learn. There are many ways to learn these skills, which form the essence of meditation, yoga and mindfulness. Teaching in these skills may be available in your community, as part of mental health services, or are available as apps or as e-learning programmes.

Once you can switch attention, start by spending 15 minutes quietly meditating, grounding yourself by focusing on your breathing. First, practice switching to a compassionate, safe image. Next, switch to situations that are associated with anger. Listen to your body and its sensations. Give it time, and you may be able to answer all of the questions below.

- Who are you angry with? The abuser? Your parent? Yourself? The world?
- Do you feel just annoyed or do you feel furious?
- Let's look at what you normally do with angry feelings:
  - Do you yell at people?
  - Do you tease and criticise?
  - Do you lash out?
  - Do you break things?
  - Do you hurt yourself?
  - Do you take your feelings out on someone else?
  - Do you suppress or try to ignore them?
  - Do you tell people about them?
  - Do you do something to change what is making you angry?
  - Do you remain passive?
  - What have you done to express your anger in the past?
  - What would you like to do to show people that you are angry?
  - Do you secretly think about the things you would like to do to show your anger?

Here are some ways that have helped other people to release and share their angry feelings about abuse. You might feel inhibited at first when you try them, but they often do work.

- Imagine a child you know or care about being treated in the same way you were treated.
- Read other victims' stories (see reading list) – perhaps you can feel angry for them.
- Go somewhere safe, and get into an angry posture – make angry faces, shout and swear, scream. Invite your recovery guide or a friend to scream with you.
- Try asking your recovery guide to sit in front of you and put up their palms facing you. Now push against them with your palms. Push hard. Get your recovery guide to push back. Get mad. Really mad.
- Punch cushions. Whacking the bed repeatedly with a tennis racket or a rolled-up newspaper is just as therapeutic and makes a great noise.
- With your recovery guide, act out situations that make you feel angry.

Make some rules about this – the bottom line being that you won't hurt anyone else, and certainly won't hurt yourself.

* Talk to your pillow/doll/stuffed toy/pet and explain why you feel angry. Sometimes venting your anger can make you aware of other kinds of feelings as a powerful aftermath – loneliness, sadness and grief. Therefore, we suggest you arrange for your recovery guide, or someone else who understands what you are trying to do and can comfort you, to be nearby.

Here are some ideas for directly targeting your anger:

* Draw pictures of the abuser. Tell them what you would like to do to them. Tear the pictures into little pieces. Drop them on the floor and stomp on them. Put them on the wall and throw things at them.
* Make your own models of the abuser in clay or plasticine. Stick sharp pins in them. Squash them. Break them into little pieces. Throw them in the rubbish bin.
* Imagine the abuser in "the empty chair". If you can't say angry things to him, allow your recovery guide to speak on your behalf.
* Listen to family members, friends or your helper being angry on your behalf.
* Make a list of the ways in which the abuse has affected you. You are bound to find things to be angry about.
* Write a letter to the person who abused you (doesn't matter if the person is no longer around or perhaps dead). We suggest you don't send this letter. It is private – just for you. Write all your angry thoughts in it. Don't hold back. Call the abuser all the names you want. Describe how hurt you feel and why. Re-read when feeling low.
* Dictate the letter onto a voice recorder.
* Re-read your letter or listen to your recording whenever feelings arise relating to the abuse. Edit, add more words, and file it somewhere safe.
* Or take it out, print your letter, and rip it to shreds. Tear it into the smallest pieces possible.

Sometimes anger can well up so much that talking becomes difficult without losing control. Try some physical exercise. Run, jog or take the dog for a walk. Try some aerobics. Jump up and down.

At some point, you may have strong feelings of wanting to get back at your abuser. You dream of revenge – or even murder. Wanting revenge is a natural impulse, a sane response. Of course, you can't act on it, but let yourself imagine it to your heart's content. This is one way of getting the hurt out of your system, of expelling it from your being and allowing your soul to heal.

Remember, being angry with someone doesn't cancel out the good feelings you might have about them. You have a right to your anger. Expressing it clears the way for you to feel whole again.

Grappling with guilt and self-blame

Many victims of abuse are plagued by the thought that they are to blame for what happened. You may feel that part of you enjoyed what happened, or that you are to blame because you accepted bribes, or that simply by going along with the abuse, you are somehow responsible for it.

NO, NEVER. No one has the right to abuse you sexually either by force or by abusing their position. Sexual abuse is *never* the victim's fault. The abuser is totally responsible for their behaviour. Nothing the victim does or says causes the abuse. Equally, the victim is not responsible for what happens to the family or abuser after speaking out.

Do you torture yourself by telling yourself that:

* There was something about you that "invited" the abuse?
* You were the type of person who "deserved" it?
* You enjoyed the special attention involved . . . or the rewards . . . or you accepted money?
* You "used" the secret to get some kind of advantage over the abuser?
* You experienced pleasurable physical feelings associated with the abuse?
* You didn't tell?
* You didn't do enough to stop the abuse?
* You didn't do enough to prevent brothers and sisters being abused?
* By telling, you have upset your family, made life difficult for them, or brought them unwelcome attention?
* You are responsible for breaking up the family?
* You have brought punishment on the abuser?
* You have behaved in destructive or self-destructive ways?

Pretend your list belongs to someone else who has suffered abuse, and you are that person's friend. What will you say to them?

Often the abuse starts at such a young age, the child is not capable of under-standing what's going on. Although maybe suspecting that it is not right, by the time you are old enough to know that this behaviour is definitely wrong, it has been going on so long, you feel you can't object or tell anyone.

Remember that children have to trust adults and can be confused easily; they always need affection and attention and so will join in any interaction with an adult. Sexual responses are instinctive and can develop at an early age.

After-effects of abuse

Different people are affected in different ways, and the after-effects of the abuse don't depend only on what happened, but also on what help and support is given to the victim. Often abuse leads to difficulties that persist in adult life and with relationships with others. Once you realise how your abuse affects you, yes, you can overcome it.

> **REMEMBER: EVERY VICTIM CAN BE A SURVIVOR.**

Get a toehold on trust

After abuse of any sort, lack of trust is imprinted on your personality. When you can't trust, a vicious circle begins. The less you trust, the fewer friends you will have and the more isolated you become. Without the opportunity to relearn that people can be trusted, you feel lonely and vulnerable and guard yourself more.

Going through life without trust is very lonely, so when you have the courage to try, take it slowly. You may have setbacks, but don't give up because the gains are great. You may find it helpful to read *The Little Prince* by Antoine De St Exupery, who recognised that love involves the risk of being hurt but that a life bereft of friendships is no life. Trust will take time to develop – be patient. Eventually, you will experience its components – honesty, acceptance and respect. Beware of romantic myths, such as those portrayed in Mills & Boon novels, suggesting that there is only one man to be with in your life, or that a "Prince Charming" (strong, macho) will whisk you off your feet (in real life, he may turn out to be a domineering brute).

Achieving the balance between caring and dependence is difficult when you have not experienced such balance in your childhood. You may need to extend the phase of developing friendships with women before you start relationships with men. We encourage you to take as long as you feel you need to feel safe and secure within yourself, rather than risk entering another victim/abuser relationship.

> **The following questions will help you work out your level of relationship preparedness:**
>
> - Do you feel that, if you depend on someone, they are in charge, and you have to give in?
> - Do you fear that getting close to someone will end up with you being hurt, and therefore you opt for the "lonely but in charge" road?

- Do you swing between feeling contempt for others and the idea that they will ridicule or humiliate you?
- Do you swing between feeling a brute or a baby?
  If you identify with any of these patterns, go back to your family tree and family diagram.
- What are your family beliefs or mottoes? Where do these myths come from?
- Re-write your story in the same way as Roald Dahl rewrote fairy stories *(Revolting Rhymes)*. How can you change the ending? Can you make people behave out of character and break the myth? Can you write a triumphant ending, or add a touch of humour? Start with *"Once upon a time there was a little child"*. Plan to show your stories to your recovery guide.

Coming to terms

Unfortunately, you cannot re-write the past, no matter how painful it was, no matter how hurt and wronged you still feel. You can't undo the damage. You must learn to say goodbye to the "wish" for better parents and continue with the rest of your life. Banishing the longing for what might have been will enable you to make room for what can be and the "real" people in your life, even if they are not perfect.

To help you come to terms with the past and to understand how this affects and influences present relationships, you may decide you want counselling. Together with suggestions for further reading, some contact details for assistance are given at the end of this book.

10 Food for thought

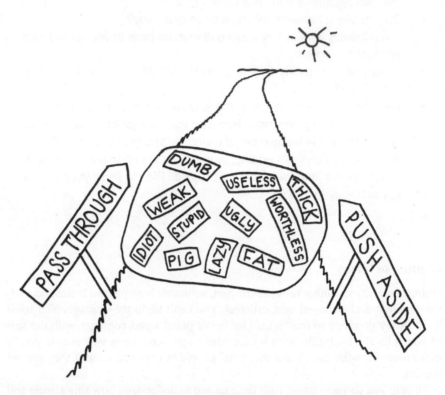

We each have our own perceptions, most of them unconscious, of how the world and people in it work. Many of these perceptions stem from childhood (that is, if your parents always told you that you are a nice and worthwhile person, you are likely to think of yourself as nice and worthwhile, whereas if they said that you are fat and selfish, you are likely to grow up thinking you are fat and selfish).

On the basis of these ideas, we try to understand what goes on around us:

> *Even though I have made a few mistakes, my friends will go on liking me because they like me for what I am*
or
People won't like me unless I am perfect
or
Unless I please people, they will guess how selfish I am.

We also use our perceptions to predict the likely outcome of events:

> *That nice boy who asked me out will probably never do so again because I am so stupid and ugly.*

Problems arise when our perceptions are not continually updated in the light of new experiences and we become stuck with a number of beliefs and ways of coping learnt as a child, that are false or inappropriate. People with eating disorders usually have many self-defeating beliefs about themselves and the world at large. Often these come from difficult childhood experiences. In other cases, the eating disorder itself can make you feel hopeless, disgusting, a mess, stupid and worthless.

Many of these unhelpful (or even irrational) thoughts are focused on, and fuelled by, the eating symptoms, for example:

> *I have binged again/I've been unable to eat enough again. I am a truly worthless person.*

Other unhelpful thoughts centre on life in general, for example:

> *My boyfriend left me. I am so unattractive; I will never find another man.*

Feeling like you don't fit in

Often people with eating disorders have been indoctrinated from childhood to believe that they are not quite right, and don't meet expectations.

Joy

> Joy had felt low about herself for years, and as a teenager, she had taken several overdoses and cut herself. She confessed that she had never felt liked and cared for as a child. She noticed that there were many photographs of her brother and sister around the house, but there were none of her. A family joke was that she had been an ugly baby and child. Her mother's friend had a daughter two months older than Joy. Throughout her childhood, Joy was negatively compared to the friend's daughter. She was ridiculed and humiliated because she was the plain, chubby one. The two families spent all their time together, and Joy could never get away from being put down.

As in Joy's case, you may have had powerful family myths built up around you (not clever enough, not pretty enough, not . . .). The scars of being the family's ugly duckling can last a long time.

Jameela

> Jameela's father was from India and her mother from Ireland. She grew up in a small village in the southeast of England.

I had a lot of trouble at school. I was often teased because of my exotic looks and somehow grew up thinking that my differentness meant I was defective in some way. Even now, whenever the slightest thing goes wrong, I tell myself over and over how worthless I am.

This low self-esteem led to Jameela avoiding social contact. She didn't know what to say or how to interact because she felt defective, that she didn't measure up in some way. To others, however, she appeared unfriendly, stand-offish and aloof and was left alone.

Do you identify with any of these thoughts?

- I don't know what to say when I'm with others, so I avoid social meetings of any sort.
- I lack confidence, and think that people won't like me, will be critical of me, or decide I'm stupid.
- I fear that if I speak, the words will come out wrong, and people will laugh.

Self-defeating thoughts like these go round continuously in your head, nagging and undermining, wearing you out, intensifying if the slightest thing goes wrong. Worse, they actually make things go wrong. Say, for example, you expect other people not to like you. You therefore behave as if they don't like you by being withdrawn and defensive. Very likely, these other people will react by treating you as if something is wrong with you. This in turn strengthens your belief that people don't like you. This is called a self-fulfilling prophecy.

Self-defeating thoughts are the root of depression and low self-esteem, and they make eating problems worse. Therefore, becoming aware of these thoughts/beliefs and questioning them is very important.

The gloom-and-doom scenario

A sense of helplessness, hopelessness and inevitability is often the result of irrational thoughts that combine three elements when you: (1) shoulder the responsibility when things go wrong (*"I let her down"*); (2) think things will be the same forever (*"I ALWAYS let her down"*); and (3) things will be the same wherever you go (*"I always let EVERYBODY down"*).

In other words, you feel that failures are due to your own doing or personality, and that this will always be the case in all situations. This is a paralysing attitude because it makes you feel you have no control over events and can't change anything. Therefore, any events over which you do have some control will inevitably turn out bad. Ultimately, this leads to depression.

When life is dreadful

Are you one of the people for whom life is dreadful? Experiencing one catastrophe, disaster, major flop after another? Maybe you are truly unlucky – some

people seem to attract problems, but if everything always seems to go wrong, especially for you, maybe this is due to your attitudes more than how things really are.

Gina

Gina always went around thinking the worst things only happened to her. Her mother was bitter about being abandoned by Gina's father when Gina was little and had always talked about how her life was hard and unfair. Gina said:

I suppose I somehow learnt to see things through my mother's eyes, to always concentrate on the negative side of things. Everything was an insurmountable hurdle put in my path to trip me up. And I'd let it trip me up. In some ways, I draw some weird sort of satisfaction from things being difficult for me. My husband is just the opposite – difficulties are there to be overcome.

People with eating disorders have an automatic bias to notice the negative. For example, they are more likely to notice people with angry, dominant faces than compassionate, kind faces. They also have a prejudice that things will turn out for the worst. In order to get balance and be able to regulate mood, the brain has to be trained to see the positive. Like all training, this takes practice and persistence.

There are many books and apps on positive psychology that describe how you can retrain your brain to focus attention on the positive.

To take steps to change negative habits, use the APT (Awareness, Planning and Try it) framework.

First, become AWARE of the balance of your negative to positive biases. Jot down how often you jump to a negative conclusion (plan to discuss how valid this is with a friend later). More importantly, jot down when positive things happen or take a "selfie" to make a record of good events. Take notes if and when you notice that others frame events in positive and compassionate ways.

PLAN. Do this by building "if . . . then" scenarios where you interrupt a negative habit by focusing on something positive or involving action. For instance, if my friend does not call when they said they would, then:

- I will call her myself.
- I will call another friend.
- I will go to my comfort box and pull out a comedy video.
- I will go to the photo book I have made that highlights occasions that I relished and for which I am grateful etc.

Visualise and vocalise some of your thought and action plans so they get automatically wired in. Let others know about your plans so they can give you a nudge.

TRY IT. Finally, put some of this into action. TRY IT again and again. You need at least 10 goes to give it a chance and even more hours to fix it as a habit. Then go back to the beginning again.

Be AWARE of what you are learning and of other ways you need to adjust your plans to break harmful thinking habits.

Wracked by guilt

A powerful sense of having done something wrong accompanies many sufferers of eating disorders in their daily life. Guilty thoughts may be especially strong after eating:

> *I reached the point where, even after eating a bunch of grapes, I'd feel totally guilty, like I'd committed a major crime. I'd know this was total nonsense and yet I'd have these pangs of guilt.*

Guilt is a hard problem to tackle.

* Try to imagine a courtroom scenario, with the judge shouting:
  *The accused has been found guilty of eating a bunch of grapes (*or whatever you feel guilty of – *eating five cream buns . . . not being sympathetic to her friend's problems at all times . . . not visiting her parents often enough). She will be sentenced to five years' hard labour.*
* How might a brilliant defence lawyer tackle the accusation against you and sway the jury in your favour? He might say:
  What has the accused actually done wrong? When did eating a bunch of grapes become a crime in this country? I admit to eating a bunch of grapes only this morning. Is there anyone in this courtroom who has never eaten grapes?

Please, please them

Perhaps you feel under a constant obligation to others. You may have a central feeling that you will be loved only on condition that you are worthy, clever, charming or attractive enough.

Self-acceptance and self-love are foreign concepts, so contentment and a sense of stability and of feeling secure within oneself become reliant on "outer" influences. The eating disorder thrives on this lack of firm foundation of self, this continual chaos and uncertainty.

The plastic pleaser

John

> John was a sensitive child; he was aware of his mother's distress when he and his brothers made a mess in the house she took pains to keep clean. He couldn't bear her cold silences, which accompanied her anger. Homesick at boarding-school, he felt it was his duty to cope. Steering a safe course was difficult, between punishment with severe beatings from the teachers for failing to come up to standard and bullying from other boys for being a nerd or goody-goody. He became highly skilled at aiming to please.

Like John:

* Do you fear not pleasing others because you might or be criticised or abused and fail to get love or approval?
* Do you please others regardless of how you feel, suppress your own feelings, and try to understand how others tick so you can maintain their goodwill?

- Are you unable to say "no" and therefore take on too much in order not to let others down, or put things off because you can't bear to get any part of it wrong?
- Do you ignore or suppress your feelings because they signal inner needs?
- Are you concerned that you may dissolve into tears or explode into anger if you let anything out?
- Are you frightened of being ridiculed or considered weak, soft?

If you have said "yes" to any of these questions, can you think of past situations that could explain things?

When you recognise that you are falling into the "pleasing pit", we encourage you to stop yourself and try to visualize how your behaviour is affecting others:

- If you don't tell people what you really want or feel, they are left trying to read your mind and divine your wishes. Of course, they will interpret your thoughts, wishes or needs at times, which gives them a profound sense of failure and deprives them of the pleasure of pleasing you. They may perceive you as being superior and aloof.
- If you always aim to say and do everything to give in to others, they will think of you as bland, characterless, without individuality; they are bound to find you not very interesting.
- If you always try to please, you will get angry and frustrated if your efforts are not noticed, and it is impossible not to let this resentment show, even in subtle ways.
- Being a silent martyr can be intensely irritating to others, as it presumes that you are right and does not give you any opportunity to see the other person's side of things.
- Aiming to please may be a selfish wish, as it may involve taking the moral high ground, but it also deprives everyone else of the chance to give and to be nice.

The bitch untamed

Perhaps you take the opposite stand to pleasing/placation as your way of coping and refuse to meet the demands of others: *"If I must – I won't."*

Perhaps, like many other people with an eating disorder, you find yourself using both coping styles – for instance, appearing all charm and helpfulness to acquaintances and yet appearing stubborn and unyielding to members of the family.

- Do you feel caged and restricted if obliged to do things?
- How does this make you feel? Furious, frightened or defiant?
- Does this attitude mean that you can't reach your full potential?

John shifted between these two poles. Mostly, he did what others wanted but, armed with the cloak of his bulimia nervosa, he could appear obstinate and refuse to do things.

How to escape the pleasing pit

Your aim with each of these coping methods is to strike a balance between looking after your needs – that is, trying to ensure things are good enough for you and doing what will please others. Initially, you may struggle to establish what you want and a formalised problem-solving approach may be helpful (see Chapter 2). As you think of alternative ways of behaving, write a balance sheet to help you define which way of coping is in your own best interest. Once you have established your goals, go back to your APT strategy to put new habits into practice. You may need to plan to use assertiveness skills (see Chapter 11).

Chant these battle-cries often to give yourself strength:

- I cannot please everyone all of the time.
- I cannot love or be loved by everyone.
- Sticking up for myself is not selfish.

When control gets out of control

People with eating disorders often organise their thinking by aiming for total control. This is due to an underlying fear of chaos. People with eating disorders have both an innate and a learnt tendency to over-control. Often this excessive control spreads into how you signal emotions to others (you don't let your true feelings show; you cover them up with a pleasing or poker face that makes you appear false). The tendency to control means the real you is concealed and you may appear cold and aloof to others.

In the following illustration, observe how too much control can be harmful:

Linda

Linda kept the flat in which she lived in perfect order. Each evening, she devoted an hour to cleaning the bathroom and kitchen. Her flatmates did not see this as an indirect message for them to be tidier and do more to help keep the flat clean. Rather, they saw this behaviour as unpleasantly intrusive in their lives. They avoided Linda whenever possible and joked about their "little housewife" flatmate behind her back. As soon as possible, the flatmates gave notice and moved out. At work, Linda's need for control and order repeatedly led her to check on the people with whom she worked to ensure that they were doing what she asked. She would attempt to delegate some organisational task but would later do the job herself, sending messages to override her colleagues' decisions. Her workmates found this intolerable; they shunned her at social occasions and laughed at her after she had left the room. Linda's obsession with control extended beyond the workplace to her food intake and exercise habits.

- Like Linda, do you have to clean or check on things obsessively or keep things in perfect order at all times?
- Sit and try to image in detail what you fear might happen if you fail to meet your standards. Close your eyes, and imagine the situation. Play through it slowly. What would you do, how could you cope? Imagine a friend whose strength you admire. How would they cope, what would they think and do? Is a critical inner voice trying to sabotage you? Tell this critical voice that no matter what happens, you will either find a way of coping, or enlist help.

Here are some arguments that may help you break free of, and avoid, the thinking traps:

- Life is not fair. I cannot control fate – life can throw up events without any justice.
- I can do a lot to improve my chances, but luck also plays a role.
- Learning to tolerate a bit of mess and chaos is an important survival skill.

The ace of self-denial

Another way in which the craving for control may manifest is to restrict our own instinctive drives. This may lead to the feeling that to have our own wishes or needs met is wrong. If we do acknowledge our need for comfort, we feel guilty or lacking in moral fibre. If we do happen to get what we want, we feel sickened by our selfishness or childishness.

Under my thumb....

If you feel familiar with these over-control habits, we suggest you use the **APT** routine to retrain this harmful habit of excess.

AWARENESS

Notice when your control habit gets activated. What are the triggers? Start by deepening awareness of when, how, what occurs; as soon as possible, jot notes, speak into your mobile, write in your diary etc. What are the consequences? For you? For others? For your relationships?

PLAN

Make precise plans to experiment gradually by giving up one aspect of control. This might mean relaxing some control over your dietary rules. Or perhaps you will deliberately leave some housework undone, for example, delay the washing-up by 10 minutes. Make some "if . . . then" plans to behave in a more open, spontaneous way throughout the day. For instance:

- *If colleagues at work suggest an after work drink, then I will say "yes".*
- *If the sun is shining when I wake up in the morning, I will put housework on hold and I will go for a walk etc.*

Think about the obstacles that might derail you when you TRY to ignore the control urge, such as overwhelming anxiety and guilt. Make plans to cope with these obstacles, for example:

- *If anxiety envelops me then – I will keep track of how long these feelings last; or*
- *I will practice slow breathing (count 10 out, 12 in) while I go for a short walk etc.*

Remember to vocalise, visualise and/or script these plans out so that they become automatic.

TRY IT

Once you have put a plan in place, ask yourself, *"What have I learnt?"* The brain learns from novelty and surprises. *Try it* – again and again. If you meet the challenge of your small experiment successfully, you may be ready to relinquish excessive control in the next area.

> You must keep challenging your excessive standards, so that you pro-
> gressively dismantle the rigidity of your self-defeating behaviors in little
> ways, every day.
>   **Go back to AWARENESS in order to put this new flexibility into
> practice.**

Victoria

Victoria was the youngest daughter of a Kenyan businessman. Her father was
very successful, which meant that he and her mother were busy and often
out in the evenings for business reasons. Victoria felt that to ask for help
with homework or to chat about school would be an imposition. Her parents
appeared too busy to be interested in her, so she had to cope alone. She felt
different to and isolated from the other girls at school, as she was the only
African in her class. She had no want for material things. Her father bought
her a flat when she was 15 and arranged for this to be rented out. From that
year onwards, her father's business concerns took him and his wife back to
Kenya for five months annually. Victoria was left to care for her sister, who
was one year older but who had a close relationship with a boyfriend. When
Victoria sought help for her eating disorder, she was crying uncontrollably,
and had a pervasive sense of loneliness.

- Like Victoria, you may describe your parents in glowing terms, as they may
  have provided you with every material comfort, but they may have neglected
  your emotional development and the need to give sufficient time, support and
  attention to you.
- If your parents treat you like an adult with a silver spoon at a young age, you
  may feel like Victoria. Like her, you may think it is ridiculous to feel like a
  deprived baby with distress. Somehow, however, despite your best efforts,
  you have an inner need that is unmet and you don't know how to meet it.
- On the other hand, your parents may do the opposite and deprive you materially to
  "strengthen you". You feel furious but can't explain or admit this when they pay
  more for the vet's fees for their cat than they do on helping you start at university.
- Alternatively, the gaping neediness inside may drive you, or make you vulnerable, to use or fantasise about other forms of comfort – eating, taking
  drugs, spending money, or sexual relationships. Because you do not understand what underlies this need for comfort and care, it seems like greed.

The semblance of power

The same underlying mechanisms can lead to the drive to create a superwoman who can be best at and tackle anything. The compulsive perfectionist strives for bigger and better without reflecting on the need or the appropriateness of the goal. Trying to give your best, if you can, is a good thing and will be helpful to you in many walks of life. However, people with eating problems often have unrealistically high expectations of themselves and the world – they don't just try to do their best, they have to succeed at being the best at all times; everything has to be flawless and just so. This can include their personal appearance, their work and their interpersonal relationships.

Ask yourself:

- Why do I need such success?
- Why do I need to outsmart or outshine others?
- Why do I need to compete so hard?

Maybe your drive for perfectionism is the result of an underlying fear that nobody will like you unless you are superwoman and that errors, mistakes, sloppiness, oversights and carelessness are unforgivable. Or you may be frightened of chaos, or feel lonely and lost without a goal. Often a less-than-perfect performance makes you think that you are totally useless, but trying to be perfect is exhausting. No matter how hard you try, it is never quite enough. Not just that – perfectionism strangles the messy, lively, spontaneous, creative side of your personality.

Society's approval of your striving for financial security, or to be the best at your job, may lull you into the belief that you do not have to question why you are so needy.

Emily

Emily became the personal assistant to the political editor of a national newspaper:

> *It was an incredibly ambitious, high-powered work environment.*

Emily did several hours of unpaid overtime every day to prove to her boss that she was excellent:

> *I tried to read his mind and do things he might ask me to do before he even asked. I wanted him to think that I was the best personal assistant he had ever had.*

However, she was rarely praised and, one day, she overheard her boss talking about her to someone else:

> *Oh yes, Emily, my new P.A., she's trying awfully hard; her work is okay, but she's so tense, it rubs off on everyone else in the office.*

Emily was shattered. You can see that Emily's attempts to be perfect were fuelled by her need to please.

Defusing self-defeating thoughts

Each time you feel inappropriately upset or act against your own interest, look for your thinking errors – thoughts that have triggered and fuelled your upset – and note any harmful habits of behaving and thinking. One way to establish whether a belief is rational or irrational is to ask yourself:

* What and where is the evidence for this thought/feeling?
* What other explanations are there?
* What would I think about this belief if I were another person looking at me?
* Am I trying to please, to be perfect or be in control?
* What neutral or, even better, positive thought can I put in its place?

You need to identify the patterns of behaving that serve you badly. "Catching" self-defeating thoughts in action can be a big challenge, as they occur abruptly and automatically. You may find that your self-defeating thoughts come from one or several of the areas we have outlined, or they may not fit neatly in any of these categories.

When you recognise a thinking trap in your own life, and there may be a number of them, start trying to notice each time it happens and record details in your diary.

* In your diary, write down the "A's" (antecedents) – thoughts or feelings that happened just before you felt emotionally disturbed or behaved in a self-defeating way – and find the "C's" (consequences) – disturbed feelings or self-defeating behaviour that resulted.
* Make two columns:
  In the first, put your self-defeating irrational belief, for example:
  I must do well or I am totally useless.
  In the second, put a rational thought, for example:
  I'd prefer to do well but may not always be able to.

Table 10.1 lists examples of the unhelpful thoughts experienced by Emily (introduced in previous pages) and the more rational thoughts she learnt to replace them with in treatment.

Table 10.1 Emily's self-defeating thoughts and counter-arguments

Irrational Thoughts	Rational Thoughts
If I am not outstanding in my work, people will see me as a totally insignificant person who isn't worth knowing.	That doesn't follow at all. There is much more of significance in a person than their performance at work. And besides, even if I am not outstanding, I can still do competent work.
To be worthwhile as a human being, I must be loved and approved of by everyone.	You can't rate a person by who loves or hates them.

- To add to this method of challenging your self-defeating thoughts, it is useful to have strategies in which you change the consequences of these thoughts, not just by replacing them with more appropriate thoughts, but by what you do. Use the APT strategy to develop plans for action with well-thought-out, ready-for use, if . . . then plots the next time a self-defeating pattern emerges. For example, phone a friend, go and visit someone, go through the balance sheet.

Next, we list some more of the argued responses to the different self-defeating thoughts shared by sufferers of eating disorders. Some are to do with eating, and some relate to other areas in life.

Eva

> *It is irrational for me to feel overwhelmed by guilt for having slightly more food than I think is right.*
> *I have difficulty eating normally, but that doesn't mean it's impossible.*
> *When people refuse my invitations, this doesn't mean that I have done something wrong.*
> *Doing something foolish makes me a person who has acted foolishly, not a total fool.*

Jane

> *I feel very good if I can keep my weight down. That doesn't prove that it is good for me to do this.*

Val

> *Even when I have a strong urge to eat, I don't have to.*

Alison

> Being disapproved of is not awful, only uncomfortable. I can always choose to accept myself, even when I behave in a stupid way.
>
> When I make a mistake, such as eating more than I feel I should, or get something wrong, this proves only that I am fallible and human.

Chantal

> With hard work, I am sure I can manage to eat more over the next few days. It will be great not to feel exhausted.
>
> Not knowing how this (important) project will turn out makes me anxious and concerned, but I will try to also use it to become more curious and adventurous about things.

Tracey

> Falling back several times and losing weight is a challenge that may enable me to learn how to accept myself fully with all my fallibility and foolish behaviour.
>
> Having lost several jobs in a row may provide me with the challenge and determination to find and keep a suitable job.

Shoo away shame

Feelings of shame, embarrassment and humiliation are closely linked to the belief that you must be perfect or else nobody will like you. To defuse these feelings, think of something you can do that is deliberately "not perfect". Defy the tug of perfectionism and exult in the freedom that this brings.

Plan to perform at least one "dare to be different" act each week, at home and when out and about. Accepting more "grey" in your life as a buffer between the white and black (in control or out of control) will ease anxiety and also help to shoo away shame. Make a list of grey ploys to employ at any moment. Feel pleased about not being "perfect" and if you feel a little nervous, say to yourself over and over: "*Perfectionism, you're not ruling me.*"

For instance:

- Sometimes deliberately arrive late for a meeting or other engagement.
- Wear your daughter's/grand-daughter's Peppa Pig hair clips in your hair to go to the library or shopping.
- Wear tracksuit pants to the supermarket.
- Send a child's birthday greeting card to a grownup.
- Purchase clothes in your favourite bright colours, and give yourself extra points for loud, clashing combinations.

- Get take-away food for the main course when the family comes for a Sunday roast.
- Get up and dance to the music when you go to live theatre or a show.
- Go out for dinner without wearing makeup.
- When out walking with smartphone music plugged in, let go of your inhibitions and skip and dance along the street, through the park.

When people look and smile, you know what to do: smile back, feel good and just "be"!

11   Finding your voice

Did you recognize yourself in Chapter 10 as someone who likes to please or be in control? Is "should" ruling and ruining your life? Do you feel drained by giving and giving and giving, until you feel totally tired out?

Do others take advantage of you because you say "yes" to whatever they ask, even though you want to shout "no, no, no"? Are you unable to refuse any favours for fear of hurting the feelings of the other person irrevocably and beyond repair? Do you worry that, if you say what you want, you will be seen as totally self-obsessed and selfish?

If your answer is "*yes*" to any of these questions, read on. You suffer from lack of assertiveness.

There are several reasons why you might have a small voice:

- You may be on the introverted end of the personality spectrum and therefore have a tendency to be quiet and shy.[1]
- You may not signal to others with your facial expression what you need or want because of the habit of over-control we discussed in Chapter 10. (This also is associated with not being able to know yourself what you feel and want – until a decision is made!)
- You may have extremely low self-esteem, convinced that you are insignificant and unlovable.

Sally

Sally is a case in point. She is a 20-year-old secretary in a small, successful company.

> *I feel nobody is really interested in me, I am not a very likeable or friendly person to be with.*

When Sally entered treatment, she was constantly trying to overcome feelings of guilt, shame or self-disgust and prove her worth and usefulness by being everything to everybody, looking after others practically or emotionally.

> *There are four girls in our office. If our boss pops round the corner and says, "Who is going to make us a cup of coffee, then?" I always jump up. Needless to say, the washing-up is also left to me. The others just won't do it. I often stay behind to clear up when everybody has gone home.*

Sally also regularly took on twice as much work as everybody else. Once or twice, her boss tried to be supportive to her by asking one of the other girls in the office to take some of Sally's load.

> *I didn't like that at all; I know he was only trying to be helpful, but I felt totally guilty afterwards.*

Is Sally a masochist or a martyr? Probably neither. However, she had adapted to letting herself be used as a doormat and found it very threatening not to be one. She feared that, if she gave up the role of "feeling used", others would reject her.

Sometimes the fear of a lot of pent-up anger or frustration coming out can stop a person from speaking their mind.

Cindy

Cindy, a 20-year-old student, shared a flat with another girl.

Although we are supposed to be equals in the flat, I don't seem to have the right to say what I think about things. Alison, my flatmate, is outspoken and often thoughtless. This has been irritating me for a while. The other day, in front of friends she had invited for her birthday dinner, she said she would not pay for a meal for me, as I would "sick it up" anyway. I was furious. I would have liked to kick or punch her or shout at her. Instead, I said nothing and gave a little smile.

Learning to stand your ground

We can communicate our wants/needs/feelings in three different ways, when we are:

1. *Passive*
   Silence our own wants/needs/feelings. This kind of communication may be given with a slumped body, downcast eyes and a hesitant, giggly or whining voice. It uses: *"maybe"*, *"I wonder if you could, only, just"*, *"It's all right, don't bother"*.

2. *Assertive*
   Express our own wants, needs and feelings, but also take into account the feelings of the person to whom we are talking.

3. *Aggressive*
   Consider only our own wants, needs and feelings. Inappropriate anger or hostility is loudly or explosively uttered. Threats are used: *"you'd better"*, or put-downs: *"come on, you must be kidding"*, or evaluative comments: *"should"*, *"I thought you would know better"*.

We all deal with different situations in these three ways. People with eating disorders often swing between the passive and aggressive poles and find it difficult to get on to a middle ground.

Think of the last time you behaved passively, suppressing your own feelings. Reconstruct the behaviour chain of this event (see Chapter 2).

A. *Where, What, With Whom and When?*
   - What were your thoughts?
   - What were the feelings (that you chose to suppress)?

The thoughts that commonly lead to this pattern are:

   - "If I say something, he/she won't like me."
   - "It's silly for me to be upset."

B. *Passive Behaviour*
- How, in what way, did you let someone walk over you?

C. *What Were the Positive and Negative Consequences of this?*

Assertive behaviour is a skill you need to learn and use, instead of passive behaviour, as a way of finding the middle ground.

Anything for a quiet life

"Why should I learn to be assertive? Isn't it terribly risky?" you may ask. Whatever your reasons, not voicing your own needs, wants and feelings may seem easiest in the short term, but in the long term, such silence can seriously damage your physical and mental health.

- Not being assertive leads to a gradual build-up of frustration, which will keep your bulimia going and can lead to other health problems like headaches and backaches.
- Other people may sympathise with the poor downtrodden you and may seem to "like" your non-assertiveness. However, they'll soon become irritated, especially if you moan about how unfair life is or look unwell with your bulimia and yet don't take their advice to do anything about it.
- Ignoring conflict might make it go away in the short term, but in the long term, tension and frustration around the suppressed conflict will increase. Dealing with situations as they arise is a far healthier approach.

You may still say: *"This all sounds like a lot of effort, and I would risk alienating people around me. I am too frightened to try."*

Nobody is saying you must change overnight to being assertive at all times in all situations, but you need to at least have the choice of behaving assertively in specific circumstances.

Ground rules for assertive behaviour

Like everyone else, you have basic human rights:

- the right to hold and express your own opinions;
- the right to make mistakes;
- the right to refuse requests without guilt;
- the right to change your mind;
- the right to set your own priorities and goals; and
- the right to judge your own behaviour, thoughts and emotions and to take responsibility for the consequences.

Prior preparation and planning helps:

- Think ahead – before negotiating, be absolutely clear what you want to achieve and what your rights (and those of other people) are. Anticipate possible objections, and work out your responses – being prepared will boost your confidence.
- Choose your timing if you can. Asking your boss for a pay rise as she rushes past your desk on the way to a meeting is not wise planning. Make an appointment with her to discuss the matter privately.
- When you make a request, be specific and direct. Avoid unassertive words like *"only"*, *"rather"* and *"maybe"*. Don't say, *"I wondered whether maybe I could be put forward for promotion."* Say, *"Could I be put forward for promotion?"*
- Criticise behaviour, not the person. Stick to facts and not judgments. Avoid words like *"always"*, *"never"* and *"impossible"*. Say something positive about the person or situation. After you have said what you had to say, don't hover. Don't undo what you said by apologising.
- When you have to say *"no"*, suggest alternatives. *"I am afraid I can't help do the baby-sitting for you tonight, but I am free tomorrow if that's any help."*
- Use the "broken record" technique on people who try to change the subject or convince you to reverse a decision. Repeat your point calmly, no matter what the other person says.
- Make eye contact. Adopt an upright and relaxed posture – keep shoulders down and arms by your side, not crossed defensively.

Employ other techniques if being baited by criticism:

- Calmly accept that there may be some truth in what your critic says, but remain your own judge of what you do.
- Negative assertion: accept your errors or faults without having to apologise.
- Prompt criticism in order to use the information if it is helpful or to exhaust it if it is manipulative.

Putting assertiveness into practice

You may have read about the importance of assertiveness before, but are still wondering how to apply this important communicative skill in your everyday life.

For situations where you can plan beforehand:

*   Practice what you want to say in front of the mirror.
*   Record what you want to say.
*   Role-play the situation with your recovery guide or another friend; change roles, take on the person to whom you make the request.

There are, of course, situations where you have to be spontaneous and think on your feet. You may be so used to saying "yes" to requests that you only notice after you have said "yes" that you really don't want that extra commitment. Remember, you have a right to change your mind. Call the person to whom you said "yes" and say, "I am sorry, but I will not be able to do the extra job after all".

You may also have difficulty responding assertively when someone puts you on the spot. You don't have to. You can tell the person later how you felt about what they said. Say, "I want to talk to you about what you said yesterday. I felt really hurt when you said . . ."

The first time you assert yourself will be terrifying, but persevere and you will improve with practice. You will find that behaving assertively leads to increased self-confidence, and that, in turn, will lead to more assertive behaviour. Gradually, your life will become more balanced.

Here we give an example of a challenging situation that one of our patients faced:

Ursula

Ursula is a well-liked, gentle-mannered person, who plays in an orchestra in her spare time. One of the other players, a girl called Lynne, desperately tried to befriend Ursula. Lynne would call Ursula daily to talk for hours about all the problems in her life, but never inquired about or expressed interest in Ursula's life. She would repeatedly ask Ursula to go out with her in a way that was difficult to refuse:

You are not doing anything tonight. That's great. I have got two theatre tickets, would you like to go with me? I will pick you up in the car.

Ursula felt overwhelmed at first but then felt intensely irritated with Lynne. She avoided her as much as possible. She instructed her parents to tell Lynne she wasn't in when she called. She thought of not going to the orchestra any more, although she enjoyed it very much. Part of her also felt sorry for Lynne, who seemed to have few other friends. She thought if she refused any of Lynne's approaches, she would hurt her and that, by accepting theatre tickets and other small favours, she had lost her right to assert herself and set limits in the relationship. Obviously, something needed to be done. It was probable that, through partially avoiding Lynne, Ursula was fuelling her persistence. The only way to free herself was to stand up to Lynne. This is how Ursula eventually asserted herself, by using the "broken record" technique:

Telephone conversation

Ursula	*"Hello, Ursula here."*
Lynne	*(slightly reproachfully):* "Hi, I've been trying to get hold of you all day, where have you been?"
Ursula	*(somewhat defensively):* "Well, I had to go out and do a few things."
Lynne	*"Are you in tonight?"*
Ursula	*"Yes, I am."*
Lynne	*"Are you doing anything specific?"*
Ursula	*"No, nothing really, just watching TV."*
Lynne	*(sounding enthusiastic):* "Oh good, I thought I might come over and see you. I'll pick up a pizza on the way. Will 8 p.m. be okay?"
Ursula	*"Actually, I don't think I feel up to seeing anybody tonight. I need some time to myself."*
Lynne	*(somewhat surprised):* "Oh, don't be such a bore. All that sitting around on your own does you no good whatsoever."
Ursula	*"I am sorry you feel I am a bore, but I really don't feel up to seeing you tonight. Perhaps we could meet at the week-end."*
Lynne	*(seductively):* "I just thought it would be nice to meet tonight; there are a few new developments with Alan that I want to tell you about."
Ursula	*"I'd love to hear about it, but I am really not up to it tonight."*
Lynne	*(more and more upset):* "I don't understand what's going on. You are telling me you are doing nothing, and yet I can't come round. I think that's really selfish of you. You don't do that to an old friend."
Ursula	*"I am sorry, but I really want to be on my own tonight."*

As the telephone conversation progressed, Lynne clearly was trying to make Ursula feel very uncomfortable and guilty. Ursula coped well by not rising to the bait and by not getting into an argument about whether or not she was acting selfishly.

Note

1   You may find *Quiet* by Susan Cain, about how to be a successful introvert, of interest: http://www.thepowerofintroverts.com/about-the-book/. This link also includes a TED talk by Susan, which may inspire and challenge you.

12 The seduction of self-destruction

Some people with an eating disorder also have problems with alcohol and drug abuse, shoplifting and/or overspending. These behaviours may simply result from the "wiring in" of wanting/craving for different substances that arise in the context of bulimia (see Chapter 4 on the topic of how alternating starving and bingeing creates food addiction and makes developing cross-addictions to other substances easier). For some people, using substances and overspending may also be a way of coping with difficult feelings and thoughts that parallel those described in Chapter 10 as underlying your binge eating.

At times, you might use these behaviours to escape the unpleasant effects of the eating disorder by numbing the feelings of guilt over bingeing or counteracting pangs of hunger. Or you might use them as a remedy for another problem – for example, using alcohol or drugs to help you sleep or relax. Perhaps you may use them to try and "cure" or get relief from an unpleasant state of mind, such as torment, depression or anxiety. From innocent casual beginnings, enduring self-destructive patterns can emerge, as you will see from the cases described in this chapter.

The slippery slope of alcohol and drugs

Strong social anxieties commonly lead to drinking/taking drugs. Especially if you "feel fat", going out may be difficult unless you have drunk something.

Chelsea

I have always been very shy. Especially when I fancy someone, I get totally tongue-tied and clam up. I start pouring with sweat, and I can't think of anything to say. Other people must think I am a total turnoff when I am like that. My bulimia has made it even more difficult to be relaxed with other people. The only way I can go out and have a good time is if I drink something first. I usually drink half a bottle of wine before leaving home. Then I'll carry on drinking all night. I often can't remember much the next day, but friends say I behave outrageously when I am like that.

Of course, if you are always drunk or drugged when out socialising, others will notice and form unfavourable perceptions, which is what happened to Chelsea.

Some good friends have said that when I am drunk, I am not pleasant to be with. I stagger about, make loud jokes that only I find funny, and flirt with men. On several occasions, I have actually got into bed with men whom I had never met before and whom I would never want to be near when sober.

Sometimes drinks/drugs are the result of the "*I can't stand it, life is too awful*" syndrome. Drink is used to ease the pain of living, as the examples of Julie and Beth show. But, of course, once a pattern has been established where your whole life revolves around drink/drugs, life is likely to remain awful and get worse.

Julie

Julie had been a promising dancer, but was thrown out of dance school because of her bulimia.

All my hopes were crushed. I hadn't learnt a thing in other areas of life. Frankly, I didn't want to do anything but dance. I had spent years dancing, thinking about being a dancer. I was so angry – angry with the school for throwing me out, angry with myself that I hadn't hidden my bulimia better from them, angry with my parents, with the whole world. Then I met Kevin, and we started a relationship. Kevin likes his drink, and soon we were out in the pub night after night. Neither of us had a job. My mum didn't like him, but I didn't care. I just drank and drank and drank, night after night. I couldn't stop. At some stage, I tried to leave Kevin. He wouldn't let me. He got angry and beat me up.

Beth

I smoke dope every day. What am I like without it? Tense, anxious, eating myself up with worry about trivial things. I am the sort of person who always finds something to worry about. I go over things endlessly in my mind – and analyse how I behaved in certain situations, what I should and shouldn't have said in certain conversations. Dope blocks all of that out. I worry about the dope, too, because it saps my energy and I have no drive, no motivation.

Some stimulant drugs, like amphetamines, help weight loss, but the price to be paid is high:

When I was on amphetamines, I was so hyped up, I could never sleep. My personality changed, and I became very suspicious.

Many slimming drugs are of this type. Many national health services do not approve of such drugs because the side-effects far outweigh any benefit.

Designer drugs

A bewildering number of so-called designer drugs are available in every class of mind-altering illicit substance imaginable. Development of these new drugs is always one step ahead of any laws attempting to ban them. Many are available over the Internet. The safety of these novel compounds is usually untested and many have unexpected and sometimes serious side effects. So taking them is a bit like playing Russian roulette.

Caffeine and artificial sweeteners

Stop! Don't skip over this bit just because you are not taking any street drugs. What about your smoking? What about your caffeine and artificial sweetener consumption? We often forget that caffeine is a powerful "drug" that can lead to anxiety, panic and tremors. In excess, your sleep and thoughts get disturbed. Putting your thoughts together may become difficult; you may get suspicious of others. We suggest you ask yourself the same questions as those outlined in the following section on alcohol, replacing the word "alcohol" with the particular "drug" you take. Again, if you answer more than three questions with "yes", you are probably heading towards being dependent on the stimulant you are taking.

When to worry about alcohol intake

If you have an eating disorder, you have a greater risk of becoming addicted to alcohol and drugs for several reasons. Research consistently finds that incidence of alcohol and drug problems is far more common among families of women with eating disorders. We do not know exactly what causes the same type of problem to run through the generations. What is passed on may be some genetic vulnerability, or perhaps when drinking a lot is your family's way of responding to problems, you grow up adopting the same way of behaving. There are also important physical reasons – like restriction of food – which make you vulnerable to the seductive powers of alcohol. Your body quickly learns that this is the only source of calories you allow yourself. This exaggerates the craving for alcohol.

Alcoholic drinks have "empty" calories; they contain none of the additional substances such as minerals and vitamins that are required for health. Moreover, the body's methods of detoxifying alcohol use up the vitamin reserves of the body. You therefore run an increased risk of vitamin deficiency if you drink alcohol. These deficiencies lead to brain damage – your memory is particularly at risk.

The safe limits

To calculate your weekly intake, it is best to count the number of units you drink:

1 unit of alcohol = half a pint of beer

    = a single measure of spirits
    = a very small glass of wine (100 ml)*
    = a small glass of sherry
    = a measure of vermouth or aperitif

* Many pubs or restaurants offer 250 ml (a third of a bottle) as "a large glass" of wine. This is about 3 units. Small glasses of wine offered in pubs and restaurants vary in size and may be 125 mls or 175 mls. Depending on the strength of the wine, this translates into 1.4 to 1.8 or 1.9 to 2.4 units respectively.

Drinks poured at home are usually more generous than pub or restaurant measures. So, in calculating your units, you need to take this into account. Write down your daily intake in your diary for a week.

You may have read that, for women, up to 14 units a week, spread throughout the week, carries no long-term health risks (for men, up to 21 units). However, as explained here, we cannot be sure what level is safe for women with eating disorders due to their precarious state of nutrient balance. If you concentrate your drinking into, say, two bouts and get drunk, you're increasing the risks to yourself even without an eating disorder. If you drink more than 22 units per week (for men, more than 36), damage to your health is likely. Your liver and stomach can both be affected. Your concentration may be poor, and all sorts of personal and social problems may be building up. There may be financial and legal problems, problems at work and home, and sexual difficulties, too.

Answer the questions in the table below as honestly as possible[1]:

Have the guts to stop or drink less

If you decide from what you have read so far that you have problems with alcohol, you should cut down drinking or even avoid alcohol altogether. Not drinking has become more socially acceptable. In some countries, people like the idea of a "dry January" or not drinking during Lent. Think of the parallel case of smoking. Twenty years ago, people who objected to others smoking in their presence were seen as uncool, silly or wet, and if they complained, they had to endure sarcastic comments and abuse. Nowadays, with increased knowledge about the health risks of smoking, it is the smokers who are at the receiving end of the criticism. This point was reached by public campaigns, but also because many people in their private lives stood up to the unthoughtful behaviour of smokers.

Alcohol use disorders identification test – consumption (AUDIT-C)

Question	Score				
	0	1	2	3	4
How often do you have a drink containing alcohol?	Never	Monthly or less	2–4 times per month	2–3 times per week	4+ times per week
How many units of alcohol do you drink on a typical day when you are drinking?	1–2	3–4	5–6	7–9	10+
How often have you had 6 or more units if female, or 8 or more if male, on a single occasion in the last year?	Never	Less than monthly	Monthly	Weekly	Daily or almost daily
How often during the last year have you found that you were not able to stop drinking once you had started?	Never	Less than monthly	Monthly	Weekly	Daily or almost daily

Scoring: A total of 5+ indicates **increasing or higher risk drinking**. An overall total score of 5 or above is AUDIT-C positive. If your score is 5 or above, continue to the following questions:

Question	Score				
	0	*1*	*2*	*3*	*4*
How often during the last year have you failed to do what was normally expected from you because of your drinking?	Never	Less than monthly	Monthly	Weekly	Daily or almost daily
How often during the last year have you needed an alcoholic drink in the morning to get yourself going after a heavy drinking session?	Never	Less than monthly	Monthly	Weekly	Daily or almost daily
How often during the last year have you had a feeling of guilt or remorse after drinking?	Never	Less than monthly	Monthly	Weekly	Daily or almost daily
How often during the last year have you been unable to remember what happened the night before because you had been drinking?	Never	Less than monthly	Monthly	Weekly	Daily or almost daily
Have you or somebody else been injured as a result of your drinking?	No		Yes, but not in the last year		Yes, during the last year
Has a relative or friend, doctor or other health worker been concerned about your drinking or suggested that you cut down?	No		Yes, but not in the last year		Yes, during the last year

Scoring: Add up your total score from both parts of the questionnaire. 0–7 Lower risk, 8–15 Increasing risk, 16–19 Higher risk, 20+ Possible dependence.

Thomas F. Babor, John C. Higgins-Biddle, John B. Saunders, and Maristela G. Monteiro. *AUDIT: The Alcohol Use Disorders Identification Test Guidelines for Use in Primary Care*. Second Edition. World Health Organization WHO/MSD/MSB/01.6a. http://apps.who.int/iris/handle/10665/67205.

Can you show personal bravery if others bully you into drinking?

Oh come on, don't be a spoil-sport, why don't you just have a tiny drink? One won't hurt.

Resisting someone who is determined to get you to drink can require much courage and self-belief. If your friends only accept you if you drink with them, and drink large amounts, are they really worth your while?

How to cut down

- Take small sips only. Count the number of sips you take to empty a glass, and then try to increase the number of sips you take for the next glass, and so on.
- Do something else enjoyable while drinking to help distract your attention from the glass – for example, listening to music, talking, doing a cross-word puzzle and so on.
- Instead of drinking your usual, favourite drink, try something new. Changing the type of drink can help break old habits and reduce the amount drunk.
- Drink more slowly, and focus on the flavour.
- Copy a slow drinker. Identify someone who drinks slowly and shadow them, not picking up the glass until they do.
- Put the glass down after each sip. If you hold the glass, you will drink more often. Do something else with your hand instead of lifting the glass to your lips.
- Top up spirits with non-alcoholic drinks.
- As much as you can, buy your own drinks. If you have to go along with sharing rounds, do not buy yourself a drink when it is your round, or order a non-alcoholic drink.
- Set aside days when you don't drink alcohol, at least one day per week, or preferably two, three or even four days per week. Take up other forms of entertainment or relaxation.
- Start drinking later than usual. For example, go to the pub later or, at home, start an hour later.
- Learn to refuse drinks. Role-play ways of saying "no" to drinks. Perhaps this is the most important assertiveness skill you need to learn. Say, for example, *"No thanks, I'm cutting down"*, or *"I am not drinking tonight, I've got a bad stomach"*.

Remember, also, alcohol removes inhibition and therefore increases the likelihood of binge eating.

Living dangerously

The sobering fact is that most people who shoplift get caught at some point. So why do so many bright and otherwise law-abiding people with eating disorders risk public humiliation, court appearance, a criminal record and, in some cases, being sent to prison?

There is a multitude of reasons for this behaviour. Some people steal food when they have a strong urge to binge, or have run out of money to buy binge food. Some take merchandise, like clothing or jewellery, that they don't need or like. Often they can't explain why they do it. The exact cause for this seemingly irrational behaviour is not understood. Starvation may have something to do with it. For example, research has shown that when people or animals are starved, they begin to hoard things. In the most famous scientific starvation experiment of all times, carried out in the United States during the 1950s, the male participants – who were deliberately starved – began to collect and hoard all sorts of objects.

Repeated shoplifting also can be a way of dealing with boredom and depression by creating a thrill. This sense of excitement can become addictive and can lead to more and more risk-taking.

Louise

I have shoplifted regularly for five years and more so since my bulimia started. As a child, I was very unhappy, and sometimes stole sweets. Now I mainly steal cosmetics or earrings. I tend to do this when in one of my bingeing phases. I don't tend to do it when I am dieting and feel in control. Shoplifting gives me a kick that's both exciting and terrifying.

Over time, you may get more hooked on it and more convinced that you will not be caught, but, of course, most people eventually are caught.

Claire

Claire began to steal things from shops a few years after her bulimia developed. She took clothes, food, cosmetics and magazines. She kept long and detailed lists of everything she had stolen:

I still don't know why I did it. I just had to do it. Shoplifting was like an obsession. It made me feel I was in control. I knew I was taking many risks, even entering shops that had automatic camera surveillance. Maybe subconsciously, I was wanting to be caught.

Claire was apprehended after several years of regular stealing. She made no attempt to hide what she had done; the police found her lists of stolen items, and she had to serve a prison sentence of several months:

Prison wasn't the worst thing. What was much worse was that the whole thing was published in the local press, with my name and address. Until then, I hadn't told anyone about my bulimia, and to have that dragged out in the open was the most awful thing.

Spending what you don't have

Overspending is another self-destructive way of trying to cope with depression, emptiness and boredom. This behaviour doesn't usually get people into legal trouble, but causes problems of its own. Many women with bulimia get into such hopeless financial situations with their compulsive spending that they owe thousands of pounds to various creditors. Once you see no chance of repaying your debts, you may think you might as well carry on and, therefore, get deeper and deeper into trouble.

Sharon

Sharon is a single mother on social security:

> *I had been feeling low and very fed up, nothing gave me pleasure, nothing interested me. I felt stuck. Then I suddenly got this catalogue and began to order things online, including several electrical appliances and smaller items for the kitchen. For a short while, I felt better, like I had achieved something. That feeling didn't last long, though. Altogether, this spending spree tallied £1200. When the goods arrived, I didn't even open the boxes to check the contents. The stuff's been sitting in my cupboard for three weeks now, untouched.*

Often the trap of overspending stops a person from getting on with what they really want to do, like going on holidays, moving house, doing a college course, and so on.

Lisa

Lisa, a typist, lives with her parents. She owes the bank £4000 and another £3000 to her parents:

> *I can't afford to buy anything at the moment. It will take years to pay everything off. I'd love to move out of home but I am stuck. There is no way I could afford to pay rent, given my current financial situation. Most of my money goes on clothes – clothes that I often don't wear, not even once. It's as if I am desperately trying to find the right thing and debilitating myself at the same time.*

Overspending or shoplifting – breaking the habit

- What is your pattern?
- Note in your diary (Chapter 2 – the ABC technique) the circumstances of overspending/stealing.

- How do you feel at the time?
- How do you feel afterwards?
- What would happen if you stopped?
- Is it that you don't allow yourself any other rewards, pleasures or excitement?
- Can you find other exciting or simply nice things to do?
- If your problem is shoplifting, some people find that the technique of imagining the worst thing they can possibly think of helps them to refrain from going on another stealing spree and committing another crime. In Claire's case, a nightmare scenario really did come true. Write down your own personal nightmare scenario, and try to imagine it every time you feel an urge to steal something.
- If your problem is overspending, you must start to pay off your debts, no matter how slowly you go. Draw a graph and watch your debt go down. Many women with eating disorders try to hide all the demands for payment at the back of a drawer but this denial behaviour won't help. A bank manager is used to dealing with this problem and will assist with practical solutions. Confide in your recovery guide and seek their guidance. Is there a friend or family member in whom you can confide about this problem? Can you get them to help you by looking after your credit cards and checking your bank statements? Can they guide you in creating and keeping to a budget?

Note and reference

1 http://www.alcohollearningcentre.org.uk/Topics/Browse/BriefAdvice/?parent=4444&child=4898

13 Web of life

Parents, partners, children and friends

At home with the family

Especially if you are still living at home, your eating disorder may cause upsets in your family. Your parents may get angry with you for raiding the cupboards or for rejecting their meals. They may feel guilty and blame themselves for your eating disorder. They may alternate between trying to help by cooking for you and buying special diet foods and angrily telling you to "*snap out of this silly eating problem*".

You may feel misunderstood, frustrated that you are being treated like a child, and that you are becoming the scapegoat for everything that goes wrong in your family. Or you may worry about the upsets that you cause. Living with other people when you suffer from an eating disorder is difficult, but living with someone who has an eating disorder is equally difficult.

Elizabeth

Elizabeth had been struggling with bulimia nervosa for several years. Her parents knew about this, especially her mother, who had read every book on eating disorders that she could find. After a period of living on her own, Elizabeth moved back home because of financial difficulties:

My mother was observing me incredibly carefully. Yet she would never mention my eating disorder. She was treating me with kid gloves. I found out from my boyfriend that she had talked to him behind my back, telling him that if he had any problem with me, he could always come to her. When he told me this, I was very cross. Am I some sort of invalid, too fragile for members of my own family to talk to? I think that my mother is so ashamed about my problem that she can't talk about it directly with me.

Improving your relationship with your parents

> • If you haven't told your parents about your eating problem, think deeply about the gains and losses of doing so. Often parents suspect something is wrong with your eating anyway, and to tell them can be a huge relief to them and to you; sharing can open the door to much needed emotional and practical support. Use the Support Questionnaire from Chapter 1 to help you think about the pros and cons of letting your parents know about your eating disorder.

- If you have already told your parents about your eating problem and their response is unhelpful, dismissive, moralising or critical, they may simply need more information about eating disorders to be able to understand and help you. Perhaps you could suggest they read this book, or use the book[1] or DVDs[2] developed to help families learn to support someone with an eating disorder more effectively or join a carers' group (see suggestions at the end of this book).
- Explain to your parents how they can help you. Remember the SMART goal approach we taught you in Chapter 1. Use this here. Be specific, direct, solution-focused and realistic. Prioritise, plan ahead, consider the obstacles and review. Positive suggestions work best. Don't say:

You don't understand me. You are getting it all wrong.
Say:
If I can eat my evening meal with you, this will be helpful. To eat one meal a day with other people will be a huge step forward for me.

- Don't set yourself and your parents up to fail by getting them to "police" you or guard you 24/7, e.g. by asking them to lock the kitchen (or not leave your side). This usually breeds difficulties and resentment for both you and them. You are likely to end up feeling intruded upon and will seek other ways of accessing binge foods. This is likely to make you feel like you are cheating and does not help anybody.
- Remember that your parents, like you, are bound to misinterpret and get it wrong at times. Nobody is perfect. (Repeat that.) Don't expect them to ask about your eating problem only when you feel you want to be asked. They can't read your mind. Sometimes a helpful strategy is to set aside time for regular reviews where both you and your parents can talk about how things are going and discuss, and re-assess, what works well in relation to their support.
- If the home environment is very stressful, consider options for a solution. Perhaps moving out is the answer. If you feel upset about living at home, do something about it. Remember, action beats anxiety.

Briony

Briony, an 18-year-old student, was the youngest of a family of four. Her father was a vicar. She had been the favourite of her parents, as she did very well at school and was a gifted piano player. When she developed anorexia nervosa at the age of 16 and nearly died, her parents felt awful – as if they, personally, were to blame. However, they found Briony's bulimic symptoms, which developed after anorexia, impossible to understand or tolerate. Raiding of the larder at night was viewed as a sign of greed and moral wickedness. Briony said:

My mother and I had a shouting match every day. We had always been a quiet, harmonious family, where people tried to talk to sort out problems.

Briony realised that her eating problem was destroying her relationship with her parents. She moved into a small flat on her own.

Once I was there, the communication between me and my parents began gradually to improve. My father actually helped me to decorate my flat. My mother agreed to shop with me once a week, as I have lost any idea of how much food I need. I visit my parents every Sunday. I feel sad when I return to my empty flat on Sunday night, yet I think this situation is the best solution for us.

Write a balance sheet on the advantages and disadvantages of living at home.

- If, on balance, you feel that moving out is your best option, think carefully about other possible solutions. Living alone in a bedsit in an area where you don't know anybody can make matters worse. Perhaps you can share accommodation with a friend.

Friends

Being able to trust anybody becomes difficult when you have an eating disorder, especially if you have been let down before. Being a reliable and dependable friend yourself can be a challenge. You may drop out of arrangements you have made with friends because food is involved. You may avoid going out for meals or to parties because that seems too frightening. Perhaps you feel so apart from the rest of the world that you don't see the point of meeting with friends who don't understand what's bothering you. Having dropped out of things a few times, you may withdraw more because you don't want to face your friends' reactions. Obviously, if your friends don't know about your eating disorder, they will get fed up with you and find your behaviour difficult to understand.

One way to improve the situation might be to tell your friends about your eating problem.

With a little help from my friends

Friends often are easier to talk to than parents. Before revealing details of your illness to them, think about how they might react:

- If you say: "*They won't want to know, they won't like me if I tell them*", ask yourself if this is really true. Or is this perception more likely to be a fear YOU have? If you are pretty certain your friends will not respond positively, maybe reconsider whether they are worthy of being your friends.
- If you say: "*They will be sympathetic, but they won't understand*", maybe you need to educate them about your problem. You can give them this book, for instance.
- If you say: "*Of course, my best friend would not think badly of me because of my eating problem, but I can't tell her . . .*" Think about why you have such difficulty confiding in your best friend. What do you have to lose? Getting better involves letting go of your problem a bit, sharing the load and letting others in to listen, guide and support. If you want to keep your problem totally secret, perhaps this says something about your motivation to change. Perhaps your desire for recovery is not as strong as you thought.

Perhaps you have told your friends about your eating disorder long ago but still worry about the effect this is having on your relationship. Answer these questions:

- Do you make an effort to look after your friendships, or do you always wait for someone else to call you? Making the first move in a relationship can be frightening. Maybe you feel: *"I don't want to be seen to need somebody"*. Perhaps you fear people only are friends with you out of pity. Remember, we all depend on others. Needing others and admitting we want their company is not a sign of weakness but strength.
- How do YOU feel when someone calls YOU? Do you immediately think they are weak for wanting to be with you? Surely not!

Making friends

Isolation, loneliness and fear of rejection are part of the human condition, but are an exceedingly common theme for people with bulimia. This is an unintended consequence of the eating disorder, as people often go on that first diet (that so commonly precedes the bulimia) precisely with the intention to become more popular with others. But once bulimia sets in, relationships usually deteriorate. Perhaps you have already lost contact with some or all of your friends or have gradually grown away from them. If renewing friendships is not possible, make a fresh start.

Here are a few suggestions to help you take steps towards meeting new people:

- Be patient. You will not make deep friendships within a few weeks. However, you may be able to generate regular social contact with people who you feel are quite nice. This is definitely better than festering alone at home.
- Don't be too choosy. Go out with people even if you think they are not likely to become a best friend. First, your initial instincts may be proved wrong. And second, these people may introduce you to their friends. Life is full of surprises when we start reaching out.
- Expect setbacks and rejections. You may find you need to issue several invitations before you get a positive response. Negative responses are disheartening, and you may feel tempted to think, *"nobody likes me"*. Remember, though, there are many good reasons why someone might not be able to go out with you. Most of these reasons will have nothing to do with you. Try to think of examples when you had to turn someone down because you were busy, tired, going out with someone else, having to take the dog to the vet, or had an exam the next day. Most people actually like being asked out, and feel pleased that you have thought of them and asked, even if they can't make it.

- If you join an evening class to meet people, as well as learn something new, expect that some classes will offer more opportunity for social interaction than others. For instance, conversation with a fellow student will be easier while doing pottery than during a math course.
- Social media can be helpful in meeting like-minded people. Sometimes you may meet in an online support group a person who lives close by and who, like you, is working on recovery from bulimia. You may arrange to catch up for a walk in a park or at a coffee shop.

Here are more suggestions on how to meet people. Think of others to add to the list.

- attend an evening class
- join a sports club
- explore book clubs, scrap booking groups
- become involved in environmental organisations
- join pressure or advocacy groups (Amnesty, Greenpeace)
- participate in church activities
- invite your neighbours over for a drink
- invite work colleagues over
- volunteer with not-for-profit organisations, such as your local eating disorder support group.

Sexual relationships

Sexual relationships are a challenge for many people. Perhaps you have watched your parents in unhappy or unsuccessful relationships. Perhaps you were sexually abused during your childhood or had frightening or unpleasant sexual encounters as an adult. Maybe this has left you feeling suspicious and wary of sexual relationships, or has made you feel unworthy, and you therefore continue to plunge yourself into sexual relationships that are unrewarding, destructive and undermine your self-esteem further. Whatever your particular pattern, you will need time to think about it and change it.

Frightened of sex

The thought of being in a physical relationship may be terrifying for you. Perhaps this is partly due to a general fear of getting too close to anyone. Perhaps you feel so bad about your body that you can't bear the thought of someone touching you. Perhaps you have been raised in a family where sex was regarded as unmentionable and not acceptable, or perhaps you have been abused.

Kate

Kate was a 25-year-old teacher who had developed an eating disorder when she was 15. She had never had a boyfriend, which she was sad about:

> *I just couldn't handle the thought of anyone getting close to me, but at the same time, I felt desperately lonely.*

All her male friends were gay. She shared a house with one of them. He was her closest friend and was very supportive in helping her recover from her eating disorder. She spent most of her spare time with him. As she began to recover, she began to recognise that the friendship was safe and rewarding, but also rather limited, and that it stopped her from meeting other people. She was frightened of moving out, but, eventually, she decided this was the only way to improve her situation and be more open to meeting someone.

If you are frightened of sexual contact:

- Ask yourself whether, like Kate, you are hiding away and denying yourself the opportunity to meet someone. To overcome your fear, maybe you need to change your lifestyle, too.
- If your fear of sex is fear of the unknown, you can take steps to educate yourself about this. You will find a reading list on sexual relationships at the end of this book.
- If you have a partner, think hard whether you can let them know how you feel about sex.

The wrong man

Perhaps you repeatedly get into relationships with the wrong partner – someone who initially attracts and excites you, but then things turn sour repeatedly in the same way. Despite your best attempts to make the relationship work, your needs are not met. You may search for, or attract, someone who displays characteristics you like but then you find they lack values and attributes you hold and cherish, and so it goes wrong.

Vanessa

Vanessa, an image-conscious young woman, who spent all her money on designer clothes and make-up, said:

> *Men see me just as a sexy blonde.*

All her boyfriends were good-looking muscular types.

> *Whenever I go to the night club with one of my boyfriends, people turn around and look at us admiringly. I rather enjoy this and all the prior preparation seems worthwhile.*

All her boyfriends are jealous of other men and, while enjoying this early in a relationship, she soon finds it irritating and claustrophobic. One boyfriend physically abused her, and another one created such a fuss in a night club that they were banned. Vanessa:

> *I often ask myself why I always go for the same type of man. I still don't know why. I am just not attracted to someone who isn't good-looking, no matter how nice they are.*

If you repeatedly get involved with the wrong type of men, ask yourself:

- What attracts you to this kind of man?
- What does your choice say about you?
- Are you drawn to people who display features that you are lacking?
- Are you drawn to people who display features that align with those of your eating disorder?

Changing your pattern may be difficult. Remember, the first step towards change is recognising and accepting that there is a problem.

Promiscuity

Many young people go through a phase of short-lived, trial-and-error-type sexual relationships. However, this pattern can become a problem for people with an eating disorder.

Deirdre

Deirdre is a 26-year-old nurse. She has never had a steady boyfriend. Since her teens, she has had many brief relationships, none lasting longer than a few weeks. She also has had quite a few one-night stands:

> *I find it easy to start relationships, and initially, I am very keen on whoever I am with. But the good feeling wanes quite soon, I lose interest and have to get rid of them quickly. A few times, I have had a one-night stand when I have drunk too much, and that has been unpleasant.*

Yvonne

Yvonne is 30. Her father, whom she has never met, was from Jamaica; her mother, who was Scottish, was an alcoholic. Yvonne grew up in a children's home, where

she was bullied. When she was 12, she was gang-raped by some older boys. She was too scared to tell anyone and became a prostitute when she was 17. She is now unemployed and lives on her own with her two children. She has never used contraception. She has been pregnant 12 times altogether. She has had multiple miscarriages and abortions.

If you change sexual partners often, ask yourself: *Why am I doing this?*

- Do you get a kick out of seeking or attracting a new partner? Does the chase and the sex feel like something slightly forbidden, slightly dangerous? If so, what other kinds of excitement do you have in your life?
- Sometimes promiscuity is the result of extremely low self-esteem. Do you plunge yourself into relationships because you feel you somehow don't deserve any better? Or to make yourself feel better? In the long run, whatever the reason, this behaviour will make you feel worse about yourself than you feel right now.
- Are you usually drunk when you get sexually involved? Why do you let yourself get into this situation?

- Do you use sex as a way of pleasing others? Is this the only way you know of gaining acceptance, of being held and hugged, and feeling wanted and loved, albeit momentarily?
- Whatever your reasons for promiscuity, make sure you protect yourself against pregnancy and sexually transmitted disease.

Children

Many women with an eating disorder worry about whether they will be able to have babies, what a pregnancy would be like for them, and whether they might damage their unborn child. We will answer some of the most commonly asked questions in this area.

Can I get pregnant?

In people with anorexia nervosa, fertility is usually markedly reduced as a direct result of being very underweight. Fertility is a lot less impaired in people with bulimia, but some studies find increased rates of needing fertility treatment in this group, suggesting difficulties with spontaneous conception. Whatever their diagnosis, some women with an active eating disorder do get pregnant despite irregular or absent periods. Some studies find that unplanned pregnancies are more common in bulimia than in other women, perhaps due to lack of adequate contraception or contraceptive failure.

Could I damage my baby?

- If, by the time you get pregnant, you have overcome your eating disorder, are at a healthy weight and are eating normally, you have nothing to worry about.
- If you starve yourself regularly during pregnancy, your baby is at risk of being born prematurely and underweight. Both these factors will make the baby more susceptible to illness. The effects of binge eating (and thus exposing your unborn child to intermittent high sugar levels), repeated self-induced vomiting or abuse of laxatives on the unborn child are not fully understood.

What will happen to my eating disorder during and after pregnancy?

In many women with an active eating disorder, their symptoms improve during pregnancy. For some, this is related to an active desire to protect their unborn baby from any harm and this helps to keep the pull of the eating disorder at bay. For others, it is to do with the feeling that their change in body shape and increase in weight is somehow legitimate during pregnancy and this helps them to relax their eating. However, after the baby is born, despite best intentions, many women return to their old behaviours. The reasons for this are complicated. The wish to get one's figure back, sleep deprivation and the stress of adjusting to parenthood may all play a role. Breast-feeding and the resulting need to eat more may also be worrying and make you feel somewhat out of control.

So, ideally, if you are planning to get pregnant, we suggest you definitely try to recover from or get help for your eating disorder first. If, however, you have bulimia and are already pregnant, be prepared for the first few months after your baby's birth to be a risky period for symptoms to return or increase. Discuss with your partner, family and/or trusted friends and your mid-wife, doctor and/ or health visitor how you can access sufficient support during this potentially difficult time.

Rosie

Rosie used about 100 laxative tablets every time she binged. The after-effects of this were terrible – she suffered severe pain and massive diarrhoea. During a short-lived relationship with a man, she got pregnant and decided to keep the baby:

As soon as I knew I was pregnant, I knew that I had to stop taking those laxatives. Once during pregnancy when I over-ate, I swallowed some laxatives on the spur of the moment, before I realized what I was doing. Afterwards, I got so worried about having damaged my baby that for the rest of my pregnancy, I didn't touch the stuff at all. Now I have got a beautiful baby boy of 6 months. He has transformed my life. I am still breast-feeding a little, so I am still not taking laxatives, but I know that when he is no longer dependent on me physically, I might easily fall back.

Will I cope with gaining weight during pregnancy?

The prospect of weight gain during pregnancy can be daunting – whether or not you suffer from an eating disorder. Many women worry about whether they will be able to return to their previous shape after pregnancy. In our experience, mothers with an eating disorder have similarly varied responses to the weight and shape changes of pregnancy as non-eating-disordered mothers. Some cope well, others feel huge.

Some pregnancy books are very prescriptive and overly precise in saying how much weight a woman should gain at different stages of pregnancy. This can be worrying and may make you feel inadequate if your own weight-gain trajectory is somewhat different. If in the normal weight range, your daily energy requirements will increase very little in the first trimester. During the second trimester, they increase by about 350 Kcals/day, and in the third trimester, by 500 Kcals/day.[3,4]

I am worried about being a bad mother

Many women with eating disorders are good mothers. However, having an eating disorder yourself can make it harder, than for other women, to feed your child. Research has shown increased conflict at meal times between mother and child when the mother has bulimia.[5] This is evident already when the child is only a few months old. In these very young children, mealtime conflict can arise if the mother tries to feed the baby too quickly, so the baby gets distressed (and if the mother then takes this as a suggestion that she needs to feed the baby more rapidly, even more distress ensues).

One interesting study showed that simple video feedback to bulimic mothers helped them to slow down a little in their attempts to feed their child and this reduced infant distress significantly.[6] Many mothers also tell us that they find it very hard to watch their child mess with or play with food and that they do not know what to do if their child leaves any food. As the child gets older, the social aspects of mealtimes, i.e. sitting down together and enjoying a meal, can also be very hard for someone with bulimia, as the following example shows.

Wendy

Wendy was a single mother of a 7-year-old daughter. Her bulimia had developed before her child's birth:

> *I have never been able to eat with her, which I find incredibly sad. She only has me, and really we should eat together as a family. But I simply find this too difficult. I serve her an evening meal and busy myself with something else. When she has finished, I quickly throw the leftovers away. She used to accept my behaviour unquestioningly, but now that she is older, she wants to know why I don't sit down and eat with her. The other day, she told me how nice it had been when she visited a friend's house where the whole family sat around the dinner table together for their meal.*
>
> *Another problem is that we struggle financially, and I often say to her: "you can't have this or that because we have no money". The truth is, I waste a lot of money on my binges and feel terrible to have to deny her things that would make her happy.*

However, it is not just mealtimes that are a problem for a mother with bulimia. The eating disorder can get in the way of other parenting tasks, too, making it harder to be attentive to your child, e.g. during play, or to set appropriate behavior limits that every child needs.

Ellie

Ellie had a boy aged 9 and a girl aged 5. She had little support from her husband in bringing up the children, as he was a long-distance truck driver and often away from home:

Both my children are difficult to control, especially Oliver, my 9-year-old. When I am in a bingeing phase, I have no time or energy to do anything with the children other than absolute basics. I let them watch the TV or play electronic games for hours while I am in the kitchen stuffing myself. During these phases, I don't manage to be firm with them, and they tend to misbehave more then. At other times, when I am not bingeing, I try to make up to the children – I read with them, take them to the park, or invite their friends around to play. I also don't let them get away with naughty behaviour. But I fear my inconsistent handling is already damaging them. In fact, Oliver's school has sent a letter, stating he is disruptive in class and directing us to see a child psychologist.

If you have children and are worried about the effect of your eating disorder on them, ask yourself the following questions:

- Are you right to be worried? What is the evidence for your worry? Are you trying to be "a good-enough mother" or are you trying to be a perfect mother? Is it possible that the thinking traps outlined in Chapter 10 might trip you up in the area of mothering, too?

If, on close questioning, you decide that, well, basically you are doing fine, other people seem to think your children are delightful and they are thriving, you need read no further.

If you remain worried about your children, writing about your concerns in your diary may help. Can you define what you are worried about? Your children's diet, their behaviour, their emotional development? Possibly, one child may seem okay while another seems to have problems? What can you do?

- Use the problem-solving approach outlined in Chapter 2 to define the problem and think of solutions.

If you worry about your children's diet, here are some helpful tips:

- Don't try to restrict their diet. Children are amazingly good at knowing how much they need.
- Don't ban sweets in an attempt to protect your children from an eating disorder. The more you try to forbid the sweets, the more interested they will become in eating them. Likewise, don't use sweets as a reward or withholding them as a punishment, as again this will make them appear overly interesting.
- Try to persuade your child to eat some fruit and vegetable every day, but don't panic if your child doesn't share your predilection for health foods.
- Is there anyone who can help at mealtimes, if you are struggling?
- There are no "good" or "bad" foods. The quantity and mix is the key.

If you find that you alone or you and your partner can't deal with the worries and difficulties you have with the children, seek support. Reach out for help. This is the most courageous and best approach. By doing so, you can save yourself and your children a lot of misery. Do some of your good friends also have children? Can you talk to them about your worries? Or maybe your doctor can help or your health visitor. Let your recovery guide help you find a solution that is right for you.

Notes and references

1   Treasure, J., Smith, G., & Crane, A., 2007. *Skills-based learning for caregivers of a loved one with an eating disorder: The new Maudsley method*. Hove: Routledge.
2   The Succeed Foundation: http://www.succeedfoundation.org
3   Butte, N.F., et al. Energy requirements during pregnancy based on total energy expenditure and energy deposition. *American Journal of Clinical Nutrition*, 2004;79:1078–1087.
4   Forsum, E. Energy requirements during pregnancy: Old questions and new findings. *American Journal of Clinical Nutrition*, 2004;79:933–934.
5   Stein, A., et al. An observational study of mothers with eating disorders and their infants. *Journal of Child Psychology and Psychiatry*, 1994 May;35(4):733–748.
6   Stein, A., et al. Treating disturbances in the relationship between mothers with bulimic eating disorders and their infants: A randomized, controlled trial of video feedback. *American Journal of Psychiatry*, 2006 May;163(5):899–906.

14 Working to live, living to work

A regular day-time occupation, whether in the form of paid work, housework, study or voluntary work, is important. The right job for the right person provides a major source of self-esteem. It can provide pleasure, challenge and stimulation. People rarely feel positively about their job all the time, but they appreciate that their work gives them independence, a sense of purpose, and a daily routine.

Many people with eating disorders have difficulties in their work environment. Such problems can have different sources. They may be due to difficult work conditions like a nasty boss, long working hours, shiftwork, low pay or sexual harassment. Sometimes people with bulimia – because they have low self-esteem or because they fear change – get into, and stay in, bad jobs. Problems can arise due to exploitation in the work environment or the job being unsuitable. Finally, given the typical onset of eating disorders in adolescence, the illness often disrupts education, with people not fulfilling their potential and either getting stuck in jobs below their capabilities or having to go back to education in adulthood.

Common work problems

I don't have a job

While there are many reasons for being out of work, some people lose their job as a result of their eating disorder.

Hazel

Hazel was 19. She had wanted to be a nurse all her life. She was overjoyed when she got into a nursing course at a major teaching hospital. However, she dropped out of the course within a few weeks because:

> *it was not like what I had imagined at all.*

Her parents criticised her decision and said she should not have given up so quickly. In order to appease her parents and earn some money, Hazel began to work in a restaurant:

> *I had to give that up, too, as I couldn't resist bingeing, surrounded by all that food. The owner began to notice that food was disappearing.*

Next, she took up a job in a trendy boutique as a shop assistant:

> *Everybody there was slim and conscious of their body image. I found that difficult to cope with, especially after a binge the night before. I couldn't face going to work in that environment, feeling fat and horrible. I soon lost the job.*

Hazel spent two months at home where her mother's constant criticisms enabled the eating disorder to get worse. Although routinely visiting the job centre, Hazel did not attend any job interviews:

> *I had totally lost my confidence.*

If you are out of a job and frightened of starting again, we suggest you think about the following:

- Being out of work is bound to make your eating disorder worse due to lack of structure and lack of fulfilment.
- Perhaps your eating disorder is so severe that you feel you can't hold down a full-time job. You may be right. Therefore, focus on doing a part-time job or volunteer work to get you going and to build up your confidence.
- Perhaps you are telling yourself that you are *"just waiting for the right job to come along"*. While there is something to be said for trying to find the right job, be honest with yourself and ask yourself whether this is likely to happen

any time soon. Maybe – and remember, be honest – you are just avoiding making a start.

- If afraid of attending job interviews, perhaps because you fear failure, ask your recovery guide or another trusted friend or family member to help you. Role-playing the interview beforehand can ease your anxiety. If no-one you trust is available, right there and then, write down a list of things you may be asked in the job interview. Focus especially on how you will explain periods of being out of work. Prepare an answer to each question, and rehearse them aloud to yourself. Do this several times so you sound fluent and convincing. Prior preparation will help you feel more confident, and increase the likelihood of success.

I am not in the right job

A lot of misery is caused if you perpetually push yourself to do things that don't suit your skills or personality. Many people with eating disorders give themselves punishingly high expectations in their jobs. The setting of often-unattainable goals may be due to your desire to meet the high expectations that your parents had, or still have, of you. You may believe that parental acceptance and acknowledgement depends on achieving these high expectations. You may have feel pressured to compote with a brother or sister who has done well. You may be afraid that anything less than best at all times equates to incompetency and failure.

Florence

Florence came from a family with high academic expectations. Her father, a university professor, and her two older brothers had degrees from Cambridge, and she was expected to follow in their footsteps:

> *Not to go to university was unthinkable in my family.*

At school, Florence had lacked interest in the academic subjects, and was unsure what she wanted to do:

> *The thought of going to university and spending more time studying horrified me. I wanted to get straight into work and earn some money. I knew I was not cut out to be an academic high-flyer like my brothers. Everybody in my family said I'd have regrets if I didn't make the most of my education.*

With much hard work and a lot of parental pressure, Florence eventually got into university and started a law course:

My parents were so proud of me, their reaction was unbelievable. On the surface, I was pleased, as everybody in my family said I was doing the right thing. But underneath, I was panic-stricken. I knew I wasn't cut out to be a lawyer. I knew I would not feel fulfilled in any way.

Not surprisingly, Florence's eating disorder, which had started while she was at school in the run-up to her A-levels, got much worse at university. Ultimately, she dropped out of her course. She got employment in a big department store as a trainee buyer. She enjoyed this work and became highly skilled at it:

I am still cross with my parents for pushing me so hard. I know they meant well, but they got it all wrong.

On the other hand, holding yourself back and aiming too low will also cause you to be resentful, unfulfilled and frustrated.

Ruby

Ruby had worked in the IT department of a bank for many years. She was hard-working and reliable. Her supervisor always gave positive feedback in her annual review. However, something was wrong. Other staff members, who had been employed after Ruby, were applying for promotion and getting it. The problem was that Ruby was too frightened to apply because she worried about making a mess of the interview. She also feared that, due to her bulimia, she might not be able cope with greater responsibility. At the same time, she resented being overtaken by younger colleagues who didn't have half of her experience:

Thinking about the situation rationally, I knew I could do a better job than they did. The longer I did nothing, the more resentful I felt.

- Help Ruby (and yourself): Write a letter describing the steps to take in preparing a request for promotion. Use Chapter 2 as a guide.

Phoebe

Phoebe was a bright young woman with an English degree. As a child, she had been her father's favourite, and he had always emphasised the importance of a good career. She felt that he was disappointed when she studied English instead of law, as he had done. After university, she had several jobs with publishing firms, but couldn't cope with them due to her eating disorder. Next, she worked on and off as a temporary secretary. She was unhappy with this, as the work seemed to lack challenge and was unfulfilling. Phoebe had a vague idea of wanting to work in the media but was too scared to try it:

> *I feared that if I tried and failed, I'd be worse off than ever. I also knew that everybody in my family would be extremely sceptical if I tried yet another new career and that I would be unable to cope with their reaction. I would look at job adverts and consider applying, but would get too panic-stricken. I felt trapped by indecision.*

When Phoebe began therapy for her eating disorder, she began to realise that she might easily go on wasting time being a temp and that her work record meant her hope of obtaining a dream job in the media was unrealistic. She decided to apply for a permanent secretarial post within a television company, as this would allow her to take a good look at this field of work and help her decide whether she really wanted to focus on this as a career.

- Imagine you are Phoebe and you are using problem-solving techniques (Chapter 2) to draw up a decision-making sheet. List the factors, for and against, that lead her to a happy solution. If your employment is making you unhappy, adapt and apply this problem-solving format to your own situation.

Workaholics

Some people spend almost all their waking hours working but not many actually enjoy such a lifestyle. If you are among those that do, you need read no further. Most workaholics, however, overwork out of a sense of battling against personal failure or out of perfectionism *("If I don't give my everything . . . I might as well not bother . . . people will think I am no good")*. Re-read Chapter 10 and try to work out what drives you to strive for success and perfectionism. Remember, overwork takes a toll by making an eating disorder worse.

Lily

Lily was a trainee accountant. She worked in a firm that expected employees to work 10 to 12 hours a day. Often she'd have to work in the office on week-ends to meet deadlines. She was also studying for her accountancy exams. She didn't have any breaks at work. When Lily arrived home in the evening, she needed several glasses of whisky to wind down, and then she would have a binge. She often felt caught in a bind and felt at breaking point. Seeking help and attending for treatment was difficult as the appointments interfered with her punishing work schedule. Lily took a long time to realise that she had contributed to the creation of some of her work pressures. It turned out that she worked harder than any of her colleagues. Because she never took a break, she was often overtired and therefore inefficient and slow. To establish life balance, Lily was asked to allow herself three breaks in the day and to eat something during each break:

This was very difficult for me to do. I had to repeatedly tell myself that I wouldn't get better unless I did this. There were always temptations to avoid having a break.

However, Lily persevered and got into a routine of regular breaks. Soon she was working far more efficiently and began to enjoy her job again. Her evening binges gradually lessened.

Sometimes overworking can be the result of an exaggerated sense of duty or responsibility.

Eleni

Eleni was the oldest daughter of a Greek Cypriot family. For many years, Eleni said, her parents had worked hard to build up a small restaurant:

They always said they did it so that my sisters and me would have it better than them one day.

Eleni worked as a nurse and lived at home. She felt to show her gratitude, she ought to help her parents, so spent all her spare time and week-ends waitressing in her parents' restaurant. When she occasionally had an evening to herself, she was too tired to go out and instead binged. Her younger sisters helped out much less. The middle sister was a student and claimed she was too busy to help, and the youngest sister had left home and was living with her boyfriend:

My sisters are really rather selfish. My parents complain about them to me, but at the end of the day, they do let them get away with it, and all the helping falls back on me.

Eleni felt unable to go her own way, as this would feel like betraying her parents.

If you habitually overwork, you may have a problem with balancing your "shoulds" and "wants". Go to Chapter 8 and re-read the section on lifestyle balance.

Is your job right for you?

> If you are unhappy with your job, go through the list below and write down all the positive and negative aspects of your job in the same way as you constructed your bulimia balance sheet in Chapter 1. As well, ask yourself where you want to be in five years' time.

Let's consider Susan's situation.

Susan

After leaving school with her A levels, Susan started in a bank on a career training course. Her eating disorder developed during this time, and she became increasingly unhappy. This is her balance sheet in which she considered the options in staying in banking.

1. *Gains and Losses for Myself*

   a. *Positive*: The income is good, and I can get a cheap mortgage.
   b. *Negative*: The work is easy but repetitive and not challenging.
   c. *Negative*: I'm given no freedom or chance to take initiative. School was better than this.
   d. *Positive*: If I stay on, I have a chance of promotion.
   e. *Negative*: With increasing computerisation and world financial changes, opportunities may be limited. Another trainee was rejected during her assessment period.
   f. *Negative*: I spend three hours daily commuting on overcrowded public transport. I have had to drop out of the local dramatic society and do not have time to go to my St John Ambulance meetings.

2. *Gains and Losses for Others*

   a. *Positive*: My parents welcome the help with the rent that I can give.
   b. *Positive*: My father likes to tell his friends that I work in the city.
   c. *Negative*: I no longer have time to help in the garden or with our pets.

3. *Self-approval or Disapproval*

   a. *Negative*: I don't like the idea that some of our profits come from lending money to poor countries with questionable leaders.
   b. *Negative*: I resent the fact that all my work is so materialistic – all for profit.
   c. *Negative*: I don't use any of the skills I know I have in communicating with people.
   d. *Negative*: I can't use my imagination or flair.
   e. *Positive*: I would have the opportunity to return to my job if I have children, and the bank would make part-time work available.

4. *Approval or Disapproval from Others*

   a. *Positive*: My parents are proud of me working in the city.
   b. *Negative*: My friends in the drama society are rather disparaging about my safe and secure but uninteresting city job.
   c. *Negative*: I hate that bank employees are the butt of so much public anger. I constantly have to face customers who are angry that the automated teller machine is not working, or that their card is stuck, or that their bank statement is inaccurate or that they have had to wait too long in the queue.

If there are more stresses, difficulties and minuses than positive things about your job, perhaps it is time to change. We suggest you sit down for a brainstorming session to sort this out.

To make an effective decision about your job, apply the decision-making steps used earlier in Chapter 2.

Step 1: Define the problem with your current job clearly and concretely.

Step 2: Write a list of other jobs that you half think you would like to do. This brainstorming requires you to produce ideas without censorship (ignore the voice that says that your father would not approve or that you are bound to fail). Include imaginative, wild and ridiculous solutions. Quantity rather than quality is important. Later you may need to combine and work on some of these initial ideas.

Step 3: Write down the pros and cons of each of your possible solutions. For some of your options, you may need to go online and research the job description and requirements.

Step 4: Rank the available options in terms of your priorities.

By following the guidelines suggested here, you will see more clearly what you want and what is realistic for you.

15 The end of your journey – or not

Having worked through *Getting Better Bite by Bite*, ask yourself: *"How do I feel?"* Answer this question honestly. If this book has been helpful and you are a good step further on your journey towards recovery, excellent! Enjoy the feeling of rest after some hard work. But be prepared for further obstacles along the way. Recovery and getting better is not about being free of problems – rather, it is about feeling better equipped to cope with and resolve them, about feeling more courageous and being prepared to try new things; it is about looking at problems afresh, about gaining self-belief, and about learning skills to avoid the traps of the harsh routines of dieting; it is about finding contentment by escaping the chaos of binges, nurturing self-respect by connecting with your own thoughts and feelings, and learning how to cater and care for your own needs as much as you do for others.

If you are still stuck

If you feel nothing has changed and nothing will change, have you actually allowed yourself to work through this book properly? Or have you rushed through it in a "bingey" sort of fashion and declared it useless? Maybe you need to slow down a little and go through the book again, chapter by chapter. This may seem irritating, tedious and too difficult to do. However, remember that the people who are most successful in life are those who don't give up when they encounter failure. So try again. Keep trying until you feel:

> *I'm where I want to be, I'm free to be me.*

Time to get real about you

You may say:

> *I can't identify with the experiences that women share in this book. My own problems are different. I can't do anything to change them. Only someone very special can sort them out.*

Possibly, you are right.

> You may need specialist help. However, even the best available specialist help can work only when you accept the responsibility and face the hardships of the journey to recovery.

Especially if you have had previous attempts at therapy and they have not worked out, ask yourself how much this is to do with the therapist or therapy not suiting you and how much this is to do with you not being ready to accept help.

The small things matter, too

Maybe the reason why you haven't been able to change anything is that too many things in your life are stressful and difficult, and you can't juggle all of them at once.

Go back to the problem-solving chapter (Chapter 2) and think again. What is consuming so much of your time and energy that you can't concentrate on your needs? Is the reason something to do with your relationships? Is it related to work? Studies? Your children? Think about it this way: builders have to do groundwork before they can start building a house, like clearing the terrain, getting the materials, and laying a foundation. Without these careful preparations, their task becomes impossible. We need to plan, prepare and do groundwork, build a foundation, for a fulfilling life, too.

Patsy

> Patsy, a 50-year-old full-time teacher, was married with two teenage children. She was also looking after her frail and elderly father in her home and checked on him several times every night. Patsy said her husband and children were very supportive but her workload, combined with lack of sleep, was causing her to feel exhausted. She previously had cared devotedly for her mother, until her death three years before.

Patsy binged several times daily and couldn't understand why she did so. When we gave her this book, she did not see how her experience related to the problems described here. She said that the women in this book were much younger, and she felt she had little in common with them. She expressed anger at being "lumped in" with people who made themselves sick, as this was not one of her problems. In talking to her, it became clear that although Patsy's husband and children were sympathetic towards her burden, they did little to help her in practical terms. For example, neither her husband nor her children, who were 13 and 15, did anything in the household. Patsy would go as far as cleaning their shoes and making sandwiches for everybody to take to school and work. Although an extremely bright and well-read woman, Patsy failed to recognise that bingeing was her only way of relieving tension and stress. She had no time for herself and was continuously driven by "shoulds". She considered the task of reading this book and appointments for treatment as further chores and pressures, designed to somehow weaken or humiliate rather than help her.

> If you recognise a little of yourself in Patsy, think about what ground work you have to do to change your life and allow yourself to focus on your eating problem. At every age, there is hope. Are you willing to start your journey now?

Recovery: An adventure in self-discovery

If you have had an eating disorder for a long time and your ways of thinking and behaviour patterns are deeply ingrained, changing your habits may be challenging and extremely anxiety-provoking, like a journey into the unknown. Or you may fear that if you change a tiny bit, you will set loose an avalanche of change that you can't control or contain.

We encourage you to persevere, for there is always a solution. Consider joining a self-help group, either locally or online, for additional motivation. Or go and talk to your general practitioner. Take *Getting Better Bite by Bite* with you. Tell your doctor that you have tried your best to help yourself, but that you need someone, perhaps a professional "recovery guide", to help you start the journey to recovery properly.

16 Where to get help and support

Knowledge is a powerful resource in understanding and overcoming an eating disorder. We thank the eating disorder researchers, therapists, carers, parents and sufferers who have contributed their recommendations to this resource list. The list is a sample of the literature and support available to assist you on your recovery journey. It provides a sound base on which to gather more knowledge, increase understanding, and seek support. And remember that new articles, research outcomes and books are emerging constantly, both in hard copy and online. Deep appreciation is extended to F.E.A.S.T. (Families Empowered and Supporting Treatment of Eating Disorders), for generously being the main source for web links listed here. Check for updates on http://www.feast-ed.org

Worldwide eating disorder advocacy organizations

** Parent-led or focused organization

International

- Academy for Eating Disorders (AED), http://www.aedweb.org
- F.E.A.S.T. (Families Empowered and Supporting Treatment of Eating Disorders)**, http://www.feast-ed.org
- Global Foundation for Eating Disorders (GFED), http://gfed.org/
- International Association of Eating Disorder Professionals (IAEDP), http://www.iaedp.com

Australia

- Australian and New Zealand Academy for Eating Disorders (ANZAED), http://www.anzaed.org.au
- Bridges Association Incorporated, http://www.bridges.net.au
- Centre for Eating and Dieting Disorders, http://cedd.org.au
- Eating Disorders Association of South Australia, http://www.edasa.org.au
- Eating Disorders Foundation of Victoria, http://www.eatingdisorders.org.au
- National Eating Disorders Collaboration (NEDC), http://www.nedc.com.au
- Tasmania Recovery From Eating Disorders (TRED), http://www.tred.org.au
- The Butterfly Foundation, http://thebutterflyfoundation.org.au
- The Eating Disorders Association Inc. (Queensland), http://eda.org.au
- The Victorian Centre of Excellence in Eating Disorders (CEED), http://ceed.org.au

Austria

- Österreichische Gesellschaft für Essstörungen (ÖGES)/Austrian Society on Eating Disorders (ASED), http://www.oeges.or.at

Brazil

- Grupo de Apoio e Tratamento dos Disturbios Alimentares, http://www.gatda.psc.br

Canada

- Bulimia Anorexia Nervosa Association (Windsor, ON), http://www.bana.ca
- Danielle's Place (Burlington, ON), http://www.daniellesplace.org
- Hope's Garden (London, ON), http://www.hopesgarden.org
- Hopewell (Ottawa, ON), http://www.hopewell.ca
- Kelty Mental Health Resource Centre (Family Eating Disorder Information Program), http://www.keltyeatingdisorders.ca

- Looking Glass Foundation** (Vancouver, BC),
  http://www.lookingglassbc.com
- National Eating Disorder Information Centre, http://www.nedic.ca
- Sheena's Place (Toronto, ON), http://www.sheenasplace.org

Czech Republic

- Czech Eating Disorder Association, http://www.idealni.cz

France

- Fédération Nationale des Associations TCA (Troubles du Comportement Alimentaire), http://www.fna-tca.fr

Germany

- German Society on Eating Disorders, http://www.dgess.de

Hong Kong

- Hong Kong Eating Disorders Association, http://www.heda-hk.org

Ireland

- Bodywhys, http://www.bodywhys.ie
- ED Contact**, http://www.edcontact.com

Italy

- Associazione Italiana Disturbi dell Alimentazione e del Peso,
  http://www.positivepress.net/AIDAP

Mexico

- Ellen West Foundation against Anorexia and Bulimia,
  http://clinicaellenwest.com

New Zealand

- Australian and New Zealand Academy for Eating Disorders (ANZAED),
  http://www.anzaed.org.au
- Eating Difficulties Education Network (EDEN)
- Eating Disorders Association of New Zealand (EDANZ)**,
  http://www.ed.org.nz

Portugal

- Associacao dos Familiares e Amigos dos Anorecticos e Bulímicos **, http://afaab.org

Scotland

- Scottish Eating Disorder Interest Group, http://www.sedig.co.uk

Spain

- Asociacion Espanola para el Estudio de los Trastornos de Conducta Alimentaria, http://www.aeetca.com

Sweden

- Nordic Eating Disorders Society (combines Swedish, Danish and Norwegian societies), http://www.neds.nu

Switzerland

- Experten-Netzwerk Essstorungen Schweiz /Reseau Expert Troubles Alimentaires Suisse, http://www.netzwerk-essstoerungen.ch

The Netherlands

- Nederlandse Academie voor Eetstoornissen, http://www.naeweb.nl
- Stichting Anorexia en Boulimia Nervosa, http://www.sabn.nl

United Kingdom

- beat (Beating Eating Disorders), http://www.b-eat.co.uk
- Boys Get Anorexia, too**, http://www.boyanorexia.com
- First Steps Derbyshire, http://www.firststepsderby.co.uk
- Grainne Smith's Working Together Care**, http://www.workingtogethercare.com
- King's College London Eating Disorders Research Group, http://www.kcl.ac.uk/iop/depts/pm/research/eatingdisorders/index.aspx
- Men Get Eating Disorders Too (MGEDT), http://mengetedstoo.co.uk
- North East Eating Disorders Support (NEEDS), http://www.needs-scotland.org

United States

- A Chance to Heal**, http://achancetoheal.org
- Alliance for Eating Disorders Awareness, http://www.allianceforeatingdisorders.com

- ANAD: National Association of Anorexia Nervosa and Associated Disorders, http://www.anad.org
- Andrea's Voice**, http://andreasvoice.org
- Anorexia Nervosa and Related Eating Disorders (ANRED), http://www.anred.com
- Association of Professionals Treating Eating Disorders (APTED), http://www.aptedsf.com
- Binge Eating Disorder Association (BEDA), http://bedaonline.com
- Bulimia Nervosa Resource Guide, http://www.bulimiaguide.org
- Caring Online, http://www.caringonline.com
- Eating Disorder Foundation (Denver, CO), http://www.eatingdisorderfoundation.org
- Eating Disorder Network of Maryland, http://www.ednmaryland.org/Welcome.html
- Eating Disorder Recovery Support, Inc. (EDRS) (Petaluma, CA), http://www.edrs.net
- Eating Disorder Referral and Information Center, http://www.edreferral.com
- Eating Disorders and Education Network (EDEN), http://www.edenclub.org/index.html
- Eating Disorders Coalition, http://www.eatingdisorderscoalition.org
- Eating Disorders Coalition of Tennessee, http://www.edct.net
- Eating Disorders Information Network (EDIN), http://www.myedin.org
- Eating Disorders Resource Center (EDRC), http://www.edrcsv.org
- Eating For Life Alliance, http://www.eatingforlife.org
- The Elisa Project** (Dallas, TX), http://www.theelisaproject.org
- The Emily Program Foundation** (St. Paul, MN), http://emilyprogramfoundation.org
- Featherweight**, http://www.featherweightinc.com
- Finding Balance (Franklin, TN), http://www.findingbalance.com
- The Gail R. Schoenbach F.R.E.E.D. Foundation (For Recovery & Elimination of Eating Disorders), https://www.causes.com/campaigns/18281-the-gail-r-schoenbach-freed-foundation/description
- Hope Network**, http://www.hopenetwork.info
- Maudsley Parents**, http://www.maudsleyparents.org
- MentorConnect, http://www.mentorconnect-ed.org
- Missouri Eating Disorders Association, http://moeatingdisorders.org
- Multiservice Eating Disorders Association (MEDA) (Newton, MA), http://www.medainc.org
- The National Association for Males With Eating Disorders (NAMED), http://namedinc.org
- National Eating Disorders Association (NEDA), http://www.nationaleatingdisorders.org
- Ophelia's Place, Inc.**, http://opheliasplace.org

- Perfect Illusions: Eating Disorders & the Family (PBS Show), http://www.pbs.org/perfectillusions/index.html
- Reaching Out Against Eating Disorders, http://www.roaed.org

Books and other resources

Recommendations from Gürze/Salucore Eating Disorders Catalogue, www.edcatalogue.com

Bulimia Nervosa

Astrachan-Fletcher, Ellen & Maslar, Michael (2009) *The Dialectical Behavior Therapy Skills Workbook for Bulimia: Using DBT to Break the Cycle and Regain Control of Your Life*. Oakland, CA: New Harbinger Publications, Inc.

Caprini, Stephanie (2010) *Living with B: A College Girl's Struggle with Bulimia and Everyday Life*. London: Lulu.com.

Golden, Jocelyn (2011) *50 Strategies to Sustain Recovery from Bulimia*. Denver, CO: Graham Publishing Group.

Hall, Lindsey & Cohn, Leigh (2011) *Bulimia: A Guide to Recovery, 25th Anniversary Edition*. Carlsbad, CA: Gürze Books.

Hansen, Kathryn (2011) *Brain Over Binge*. Columbus, GA: Camellia Publishing.

McCabe, Randi (2003) *The Overcoming Bulimia Workbook: Your Comprehensive Step-by-Step Guide to Recovery*. Oakland, CA: New Harbinger Publications, Inc.

Miller, Caroline (2013) *Positively Caroline: How I Beat Bulimia for Good . . . and Found Real Happiness*. Putnam Valley, NY: Cogent Publishing.

Sandoz, E., Wilson, K. & DuFrene, T. (2011) *The Mindfulness and Acceptance Workbook for Bulimia: A Guide to Breaking Free from Bulimia Using Acceptance and Commitment Therapy*. Oakland, CA: New Harbinger Publications, Inc.

Smeltzer, Doris (2006) *Andrea's Voice: Silenced by Bulimia*. Carlsbad, CA: Gürze Books.

Professional treatment

Le Grange, Daniel & Lock, James (2007) *Treating Bulimia in Adolescents: A Family-Based Approach*. New York, NY: The Guilford Press.

Safer, D., Telch, C. & Chen, E. (2009) *Dialectical Behavior Therapy for Binge Eating and Bulimia*. New York, NY: The Guilford Press.

Zweig, Rene & Leahy, Robert (2012) *Treatment Plans and Interventions for Bulimia and Binge-Eating Disorder*. New York, NY: The Guilford Press.

General

Agras, W. Stewart & Apple, Robin (2008) *Overcoming Eating Disorders, Second Edition: A Cognitive-Behavioral Therapy Approach for Bulimia Nervosa and Binge-Eating Disorder Therapist Guide*. New York, NY: Oxford University Press, Inc.

Grilo, Carlos & Mitchell, James (2010) *The Treatment of Eating Disorders: A Clinical Handbook*. New York, NY: The Guilford Press.

Lask, Bryan & Frampton, Ian (2011) *Eating Disorders and the Brain.* Hoboken, NJ: John Wiley and Sons.

Lask, Bryan & Watson, Lucy (2014) *Can I tell you about Eating Disorders? A Guide for Friends, Family and Professionals.* London: Jessica Kingsley Publishing.

LeGrange, Daniel & Lock, James (2011) *Eating Disorders in Children and Adolescents: A Clinical Handbook.* New York, NY: The Guilford Press.

Maine, M., Davis, W. & Shure, J. (2009) *Effective Clinical Practice in the Treatment of Eating Disorders: The Heart of the Matter.* New York, NY: Routledge, Taylor & Francis Group.

Maine, M., McGilley, B. & Bunnell, D. (2010) *Treatment of Eating Disorders: Bridging the Research-Practice Gap.* London, UK: Elsevier Inc.

Mehler, Philip & Andersen, Arnold (1999) *Eating Disorders: A Guide to Medical Care and Complications, Second Edition.* Baltimore, MD: The Johns Hopkins University Press.

Sandoz, E., Wilson, K. & Dufrene, T. (2010) *Acceptance and Commitment Therapy for Eating Disorders: A Process-Focused Guide to Treating Anorexia and Bulimia.* Oakland, CA: New Harbinger Publications, Inc.

Zerbe, Kathryn (2008) *Integrated Treatment of Eating Disorders: Beyond the Body Betrayed.* New York, NY: W.W. Norton & Company, Inc.

Online sites to explore to assist self-renewal and healing

http://www.cci.health.wa.gov.au/resources/consumers.cfm
https://www.graceonthemoon.com

Further reading

Titles by Ulrike Schmidt, Janet Treasure and June Alexander

Alexander, June (2015) *Using Writing as a Resource to Treat Eating Disorders: The diary healer.* Hove: Routledge.

Alexander, June et al. (2013) *A Clinician's Guide to Binge Eating Disorder.* Hove: Routledge.

Alexander, June & Sangster, Cate (2013) *ED says U said – Eating Disorder Translator.* London: Jessica Kingsley Publishers.

Alexander, June & Treasure, Janet (2011) *A Collaborative Approach to Eating Disorders.* Hove: Routledge.

Schmidt, Ulrike & Davidson, Kate (2004) *When Life Is too Painful. A Self-help manual for individuals who have harmed themselves.* Hove, East Sussex: Psychology Press.

Taylor, Lucy, Simic, Mima & Schmidt, Ulrike (2015) *Cutting Down: A CBT workbook for treating young people who self-harm.* Hove, East Sussex: Routledge.

Treasure, Janet (1997) *Anorexia Nervosa: A Survival Guide for Sufferers and those Caring for Someone with an Eating Disorder.* Hove: Psychology Press.

Treasure, Janet & Alexander, June (2013) *Anorexia Nervosa, A Recovery Guide for Sufferers, Families and Friends, Second edition.* Hove: Routledge.

Treasure, Janet et al. (2007) *Skills-based Learning for Caring for a Loved One with an Eating Disorder: The New Maudsley Method.* Hove: Routledge.

Anorexia nervosa – its effect on the brain

Arnold, Carrie (2012) *Decoding Anorexia – How Breakthroughs in Science Offer Hope for Eating Disorders*: Hove: Routledge.
Lask, Bryan & Frampton, Ian (2011) *Eating Disorders and the Brain*. Chichester: Wiley.

Parents

Bevan, Charlotte & Collins Lyster-Mensh, Laura (2013) *Throwing Starfish Across the Sea*. Biscotti Press.
Brown, Harriet (2010) *Brave Girl Eating*. New York: William Morrow.
Collins, Laura (2015) *Eating with Your Anorexic: A Mother's Memoir*. Biscotti Press.
Hamilton, Fiona (2014) *Bite Sized: A mother's journey alongside anorexia*. Bristol: Vala Publishers.
Henry, Becky (2011) *Just Tell Her To Stop: Family Stories of Eating Disorders*. Carol Stream, IL: Infinite Hope Publishing.

Education – schools

Atkinson, M. & Hornby, G. (2002) *Mental Health Handbook for Schools*. Hove: Routledge.
Capuzzi, D. & Gross, D.R. (2008) *Youth at Risk: A Prevention resource for Counselors, Teachers, and Parents*. Alexandria, VA: American Counseling Association.
Cook-Cottone, C. (2009) Eating disorders in childhood: Prevention and treatment supports. *Childhood Education*, 85, 5: 300.
Favaro, A., Zanetti, T., Huon, G. & Santonastaso, P. (2005) Engaging teachers in an eating disorder preventive intervention. *The International Journal of Eating Disorders*, 38, 1: 73–77.
Knightsmith, P. (2012) *Eating Disorders Pocketbook*. Hampshire: Teachers' Pocketbooks.
Prever, M. (2006) *Mental Health in Schools – A Guide to Pastoral and Curriculum Provision*. London: Paul Chapman Publishing.
Yager, Z. & O'Dea, J. (2010) A controlled intervention to promote a healthy body image, reduce eating disorder risk and prevent excessive exercise among trainee health education and physical education teachers. *Health Education Research*, 25, 5: 841–852.

Online sites

This website provides eating disorders support and advice aimed at teachers: www.eatingdisordersadvice.co.uk
This link provides a model eating disorders policy that can be adapted for use in your school: www.eatingdisordersadvice.co.uk/policy

General

American Academy of Pediatrics. Committee on Adolescence (2003) Identifying and treating eating disorders. *Pediatrics*, 111, 1: 204–211.
Costin, C. (2007) *The Eating Disorder Sourcebook: A Comprehensive Guide to the Causes, Treatments, and Prevention of Eating Disorders*. New York: McGraw-Hill.

Lask, B. & Bryant-Waugh, R. (2007) *Eating Disorders in Childhood and Adolescence.* Hove: Routledge.
Michel, D.M. & Willard, S.G. (2003) *When Dieting Becomes Dangerous: A Guide to Understanding and Treating Anorexia and Bulimia.* New Haven: Yale University Press.
Schwartz, Jeffrey with Beyette, Beverley (1996) *Brain Lock: Free Yourself from Obsessive-Compulsive Behaviour.* London: HarperCollins.

Stories of survival, regaining and restoring life

Alexander, June (2011) *A Girl Called Tim – Escape from an Eating Disorder Hell.* London: New Holland.
Cutts, Shannon (2009) *Beating Ana – How to Outsmart your Eating Disorder and Take Your Life Back.* Deerfield Beach, FL: Health Communications Inc.
Liu, Aimee (2007) *Gaining – The Truth About Life After Eating Disorders.* New York: Warner Books.
Liu, Aimee (2011) *Restoring Our Bodies, Reclaiming Our Lives: Guidance and Reflections on Recovery from Eating Disorders.* London: Trumpeter Books.
Schaefer, Jenni with Rutledge, Thom (2014) Life Without Ed: How One Woman Declared Independence from Her Eating Disorder and How You Can Too. New York, NY: McGraw-Hill. An audiobook is also available: Recorded by Jenni Schaefer, Life Without Ed, Tenth Anniversary Edition. Grand Haven, MI: Brilliance Audio, 2014.
Schaefer, Jenni (2009) Goodbye Ed, Hello Me: Recover from Your Eating Disorder and Fall in Love with Life. New York, NY: McGraw-Hill.
Thomas, Jennifer J. & Schaefer, Jenni (2013) *Almost Anorexic: Is My (or My Loved One's) Relationship with Food a Problem?* Center City, MN: Hazelden.

Eating disorders in midlife

Bulik, Cynthia (2013) *Midlife Eating Disorders: Your Journey to Recovery.* London: Walker Publishing.

Dieting culture, body image, feminist texts

Bacon, Linda (2008) *Health at Every Size.* Dallas, TX: BenBella Books Inc.
Bulik, Cynthia (2009) *Crave – Why You Binge and How to Stop.* London: Walker Publishing.
Bulik, Cynthia (2011) *Woman in the Mirror – How to Stop Confusing What You Look Like with Who You Are.* London: Walker Publishing.
Forbush, K., Heatherton, T. & Keel, P. (2007) Relationships between perfectionism and specific disordered eating behaviors. *International Journal of Eating Disorders*, 40: 37–41.
Frankel, Ellen & Matz, Judith (2004) *Beyond a Shadow of a Diet – The Therapist's Guide to Treating Compulsive Eating.* Hove: Brunner-Routledge.
Gaesser, Glen (2002) *Big Fat Lies – The Truth About Your Weight and Health.* Carlsbad, CA: Gurze Books.
Hayaki, J., Friedman, M.A., Whisman, M.A., Delinsky, S.S. & Brownell, K.D. (2003) Sociotropy and bulimic symptoms in clinical and nonclinical samples. *International Journal of Eating Disorders*, 34: 172–176.

Katrina, Karin, King, Nancy & Hayes, Dayle (2003) *Moving Away from Diets – Healing Eating Problems and Exercise Resistance*. London: Helm Publishing.

Kilbourne, Jean (1999) *Can't Buy My Love*. New York: Touchstone.

Matz, Judith & Frankel, Ellen (2006) *The Diet Survivor's Handbook*. Naperville, IL: Sourcebooks.

Michel, Deborah Marcontell & Willard, Susan G. (2003) *When Dieting Becomes Dangerous*. New Haven: Yale University Press.

Neumark-Sztainer, Dianne (2005) *I'm, Like, SO Fat*. New York: Guildford Press.

Nilsson, K., Sundbom, E. & Hagglof, B. (2008) A longitudinal study of perfectionism in adolescent onset anorexia nervosa-restricting type. *European Eating Disorders Review*, 16: 386–394.

Roth, Geneen (2011) *Women, Food & God: An Unexpected Path to Almost Everything*. New York: Scribner.

Sansone, R.A. & Sansone, L.A. (2011). Personality pathology and its influence on eating disorders. *Clinical Neuroscience*, 8: 14–18.

Professional

Malson, Helen & Burns, Maree (2009) *Critical Feminist Approaches to Eating Disorders*. Hove: Routledge.

Disordered eating

Ross, Carolyn (2009) *The Binge Eating and Compulsive Overeating Workbook: An Integrated Approach to Overcoming Disordered Eating*. Oakland, CA: New Harbinger Publications.

Recovery

Birgegard, A., Bjorck, C., Norring, C. Sholberg, S. & Clinton, D. (2009) Anorexic Self-Control and Bulimic Self-Hate: Differential Outcome Prediction from Initial Self-Image. *International Journal of Eating Disorders*, 46, 6: 522–530.

Cabrera, Dena & Wierenga, Emily (2013) *Mom in the Mirror: Body Image, Beauty, and Life After Pregnancy*. Lanham, MD: Rowman and Littlefield.

Costin, Carolyn & Schubert Grabb, Gwen (2011) *8 Keys to Recovery from an Eating Disorder: Effective Strategies from Therapeutic Practice and Personal Experience*. London: W.W. Norton and Company.

Johnston, Anita (2000*) Eating in the Light of the Moon: How Women Can Transform their Relationships with Food Through Myths, Metaphors and Storytelling*. Carlsbad, CA: Gurze Books.

Maine, Margo with Kelly, Joe (2005) *The Body Myth: Adult Women and the Pressure to Be Perfect*. Chichester: John Wiley.

Siegel, Michele, Brisman, Judith & Weinshel, Margot (2009) *Surviving an Eating Disorder: Strategies for Family and Friends*. Bloomington, IN: First Collins Living.

Tribole, Evelyn & Resch, Elyse (2012) *Intuitive Eating, Third edition.* New York: St Martin's Griffin.

Weight stigma

Puhl, Rebecca, Rudd Center, Yale. *Weight Bias and Stigma.* www.yaleruddcenter.org/what_we_do.aspx?id=10 (accessed 27 May 2014).

Appendix
Food Diary

Time	What eaten	B	V	L	Antecedents and consequences

B = Binge, V = Vomited, L = Laxatives

Weekly reflection box:

Looking over your diary from this week:

What went well and why?

What progress did you make towards your goal(s)?

How can you build on this?

What did not go so well and why?

What obstacles occurred?

How can you reduce or prevent this from happening again?

What are the next steps for you to take over the coming week?
[Remember keep goals realistic and achievable.]
My goals for this coming week are:

1.
2.
3.